Shipwrecks and Bush Felling

Shipwrecks and Bush Felling

Originally penned by
George Richard Meredith

Rewritten by
Wendy Hamilton

ZealAus Publishing

Shipwrecks and Bush Felling
New Zealand Pioneer Able Seaman G.R. Meredith

Copyright © 2020 by Wendy Hamilton

www.zealauspublishing.com

All rights reserved. No part of this book may be reproduced or transmitted in any form or by any means without written permission of the author. Attitudes expressed in this book are not necessarily the attitudes of Wendy Hamilton or ZealAus Publishing.

Modified Cover Images by Adobe Stock Images Some of the internal images were sourced from "Sunday at Home" from years 1874 and 1880.

ISBN: 978-1-925888-62-1 (e)
ISBN: 978-1-925888-63-8 (hc)
ISBN: 978-1-925888-64-5 (sc)

Dedicated
to
George Richard Meredith's descendants.

Contents

The Adventures Begin 1
My Second Voyage. 12
Out to Sea Again. 18
A Secret Cargo 21
A Princess and a Sea Chase 29
Shipwreck. 34
Disaster. 37
Adrift at Sea 44
The Darkest Hour 47
Homeward Bound. 51
Homecoming 55
Onboard the Prince. 59
Runaways 65
America 73
Goodbye England 77
Sailor's Hell 82
Escape and New Friends 87
Gold Fever 92
Health Troubles and a Doctor's Advice 96
Goodbye to Life at Sea. 99
New Zealand. 102
Searching for Work. 109
Bush Felling 119
My Family Arrives in New Zealand 125
Shin Plasters 129
Bridge Building 133
The Last of my Single Years 136
Marriage 141

Married Life	146
Lime Burning	152
Railway Work	157
Coal	162
Milling Again	165
Journey's End	171
Obituary	174
Shipping Records	176
Descendents	182

October 18th 1910

Rocky Point
Kakahu
Geraldine NZ

Since I have been asked by many kind friends to write the story of my life, I am making a beginning, but whether I shall live long enough to finish it, I don't know.

I am 76 years of age, and my life has been a very rough one. I have travelled all over the world, except India, and have learned all I know myself. So I can claim to be a self taught man and have come out alright by long practice, in every trade I tackled, such as sailor for nine years in my boyhood days.

Leaving the sea at twenty one years old, for the gold diggings, I got sand blight in my eyes and was advised by Doctor to clear out, which I did, and came to New Zealand 55 years ago, where I have learned many trades, such as Pit sawing, Sawmilling, making my own furniture, building my own houses from standing trees to finished building. Also Wheelwright, Blacksmith, building my own Saw Mills, Engineering, and Lime burning which I liked best of all trades, and made more money, but had to work day and night to keep things going. I worked also at Road making and Farming but did not like the work.

                George Richard Meredith

Forward

Shipwrecks and Bush Felling is an interesting and readable narrative. I think it is important to preserve these personnel accounts as they illustrate and fill in the broader trends of history. Although he didn't realise it George's voyages show how the process of ship owning was changing. And his later career as a pioneer in New Zealand shows how the development of that country's economy generated different needs. George was certainly aware of how this impacted on his livelihood and was quick to adapt. He was a tough, self-made, and resourceful man. His sea faring career, including going to sea at a very early age, the varied nature of his ships and voyages, the casual nature of the employment, and the progression upwards as experience was gained and recognized, is typical of the era. His memories are clear after some sixty years although the timing may occasionally be out. He may still have had his discharge papers available to jog his memory. His voyages should also be recorded in the British Archives. From the 1830s onwards the Government started a more systematic regulation of the Merchant Service. Part of this was an attempt to keep an index of seafarers. Several series of index card were kept up until 1857 when it was decided that it was too difficult to manage. Some decades later seafarers were issued with Discharge Books that recorded each voyage. I still remember the number of mine: R564306. Congratulations Wendy for producing a fitting tribute to George Richard Meredith. I hope your other readers get to know him as well as I did.

Ron Hawkins, retired Master Mariner

Introduction

This book is a joint project between myself and George Richard Meredith; a man I have never met and yet I owe my existence to. He is my great, great, grandfather, and this book is based on his autobiography written in 1913 called the Life and Adventures of George Richard Meredith. Without his memoir this book would not exist. Without me it would have stayed hidden in the South Canterbury Museum. I have tried to use George Meredith's own words and narrative where possible and think he would approve of the additions and changes I have made. For I feel sure he would rather school boys read his story than it is hidden away in dusty archives. Some of George's attitudes towards the Africans and the New Zealand bush are offensive to the twenty-first-century way of thinking. The temptation is to remove or alter the text. I have not done this, however, as I have been working off a historical document and wish to retain the mindset of the time. So, without further ado, my grandfather and I jointly present to you the Life and Adventures of George Richard Meredith, who sailed the seas and became a beloved New Zealand pioneer.

Wendy Hamilton

I was born on September the 1st 1834.

G.R. Meredith / W.E. Hamilton

The Adventures Begin

I was born on September the first, 1834 in Crown Street, Finsbury, in the Parish of Shoreditch, London, the thirteenth child of John and Mary Meredith. Twenty days later I was baptized into the Church of England at St Leonard's on High Street. I was six when Britain and the Maori Chiefs of New Zealand signed the treaty of Waitangi; although at that time, this historic event meant nothing to me. For the distant nation was unknown to me, and my chances of living anywhere other than Shoreditch were slim, as expectations to follow in my father's footsteps were strong. Far more important was the small birthday cake my mother baked me every year.

When I was five years old, my parents shifted to Halwell Road, Worship Street, Finsbury, and very happy I was there with my dear old father and mother. Shoreditch was a busy place in those days. The opening of the Regents Canal in 1820 made timber transportation cheaper and easier, and

Shipwrecks and Bush Felling

new furniture factories seemed to be opening every week. I knew my way around the crowded streets as well as any boy and often wandered down to the river to watch the boats that passed. But back then I had no thoughts of going to sea.

I often wandered down to the river to watch the boats.

It was not until 1845 when I was eleven, I suddenly became sea mad through one of my school mates arriving home from a voyage, dressed in a sailor's rigout. I thought his uniform looked very smart, and there and then, I made up my mind to go to sea. But by then I was grown into a big strong boy and was becoming very useful to my father at his trade of blind making.

"Why do you want to go to sea, my boy?" Dad said. "You'll have all manner of miseries if you go to sea. Why not stay here and have a comfortable life as a blind maker?"

But blind making, to an eleven-year-old boy, seemed tame compared to a sailor's suit and exotic lands.

When my father saw I was not persuaded, he tried another tack.

"Think of your mother and me, and your brother and sister. You are not old enough to remember the big plague of 1830 but Magnus and Mary Anne are. Ten of your siblings were lost, would you break our hearts by drowning at sea?"

With these and other persuasions my father tried hard to keep me from going, but it was no use, the dazzle of my friend's sailor suit had me in its grip and go I must. It grieves me when I think of dear old Dad, for I know he loved me very dearly.

My trouble was how to get a chance to go to sea, since Dad would not help me and tried hard to stop me. But as Shoreditch abounded with furniture factories I rebelled and got a strong boy's place at nineteen shillings a week. It was not the sea but at least it was not blind making.

When my father saw I would not go into the family business, he said:

"Well son, if you won't give up this foolish notion of going to sea, I will make you a deal. I have a large order from a shipowner called Mr. McNultin. I have to fix binds at his

Shipwrecks and Bush Felling

shipping office. Come and help me and I will talk to him about you going to sea."

So, I gave up my job and went with my father to fix the blinds.

My father, being a man of his word, had a private talk with Mr. McNultin.

"My son is mad about going to sea," he said.

"Let him go," said Mr. McNultin, "for you will be able to do nothing with him if you keep him from going."

When we had finished our work, the owner came to inspect both the blinds and me.

"Is this the lad who's keen on going to sea?" he asked, looking me over.

"Yes," I answered, "I would very much like to go to sea."

"Do you have a ship needing a boy?" asked my father.

"Only one, but it is going to Sierra Leone," he said. "I'll be honest with you, Sierra Leone is the white man's grave with fevers and all manner of diseases."

At this my father looked troubled, but I spoke up and said; "that doesn't matter as there is the same God there as anywhere else."

It must have been the right thing to say for Mr. McNultin turned to my father and said: "He'll do, let him go. I'll write a letter of recommendation for George to take to Captain Fraser."

The next day I went to see Captain Fraser and a fine man he was. He read the letter I gave him and sized me up with piercing eyes.

"You look very young and not big enough for a cabin boy," he said, "but as you are recommended by Mr. McNultin, I will ship you for the voyage, and if you suit, you can be apprenticed.

G.R. Meredith / W.E. Hamilton

My father had a private talk with Mr. McNultin.

My ship is the London of London, a barque of 239 tons. It's going to Sierra Leone to pick up oak logs for the Government. Your pay will be ten shillings a month for the voyage."

"Thank you, Sir," I said.

I stood there while he wrote a letter and sealed it.

"Take this back to Mr. McNultin," he said, handing it to me.

I took the letter and you may be sure it was not long before Mr. McNultin got it. After delivering the note I made for home

Shipwrecks and Bush Felling

and could not get there fast enough to tell them of my good fortune. Seeing a cab going near my house, I took my chance when the driver was not looking, and leapt up behind it, and so got a cheap ride home.

Shortly thereafter my father got a letter from the owner to say when the old London would sail. When all was fixed up, I finally had my sailor's outfit and very grand I felt in my new rigout and smart hat.

My family came to see me off from the London dock.

"Goodbye Thomas and Charles," I said, kissing my small brothers. They being five and three thought nothing of the possible perils that lay before me. But my mother and sister clung to me and wept.

"Now then, Mother," said Dad, at last. "We must let him forge his way in the world and trust the Lord will be with him."

Then he hugged me, and my brother Magnus (who was twenty-five and above such things) shook my hand.

I walked up the gangway jauntily and felt quite the man as the tug boat got hold of us and pulled us away. The old ship looked magnificent with all her sails up when we got to open sea. A good breeze sprang up and the trip was uneventful, although to a lad of my age everything was new and unusual. The ship possessed me completely, and a hundred times a day I gazed up at the billowing sails in delight. Yet despite this, homesickness overwhelmed me at times. Captain Fraser was like a father to me and I shall never forget him and his kindness and consideration for a lonely lad. By the time we had been at sea for three months, I was eager to catch a glimpse of the West coast of Africa. When at last we docked at Sierra Leone, I felt like I was in another world it, was so vastly different to the streets of Shoreditch. The heat was so intense that the captain hired native crew-boys to thatch the decks with palm leaves.

I was eager to catch my first glimpse of Africa.

"Why are they doing that?" I asked one of my shipmates.

"It helps keep the fever down and stops the sun from burning the decks," he said grimly.

I was not so certain of my brave words to Mr. McNultin now that I was faced with the realities of The-White-Man's-

Shipwrecks and Bush Felling

Grave. What with the heat and the diseased air, it was more like a floating hell than anything I could have imagined. We had a lot of trouble with the crew on account of the fever, which was very bad. This is where I now see God's hand watching over me. I did not get sick. My worst affliction was loneliness and I spent my twelfth birthday at Sierra Leone crying to see my mother.

Captain Fraser (God bless him) said, "what are you crying for lad, have you got the fever?"

"No, nothing like that," I said wiping my eyes, "it is my birthday and my mother always made me a cake."

"Is that all, my boy, go and see the steward in the cabin and tell him the captain says to fix you up with a cake."

I did as he bid and the steward made me a capital cake which cheered me up immensely. As I ate my cake, I envied the crew-boys for they were always in the water.

"Why do they lash brushwood onto the logs," I asked a shipmate, as I watched the coolies float the logs alongside the vessel and into position under the bows.

"It is African oak we are loading on board," he said. "African oak will not float. See how once the chains are fastened around the logs, the crew-boys cut the brushwood off them."

And indeed, it was so. After the chain was fastened to the log and the brushwood removed, the log was pulled in through the porthole in the bow of the ship, and shortly after, disappeared out of sight.

Once my cake was eaten, it was time to get back to work.

While the cargo was being loaded my job was to keep the decks clear and hand the men ropes, and blocks, tar-pots, and anything else they wanted, as they were making new gear for standby during the passage home. What with the fierce heat and the fear of the fever, it was a trying time for me at that age. I had to clear up everything by eleven o'clock and strike seven bells when the men went below.

One day two men were missing, so I went to the cabin door and knocked on it.

"Yes, what do you want," said the mate.

"Please, Sir, two of the men are missing."

"Missing?" he said, coming out.

"Yes, missing, Sir."

"Well, we'd better go look for them."

We searched the deck and found them in the corner dead. We all felt those deaths very much for they were noble sailors and none of us knew how soon our turn would come.

"The quicker we can get loaded and out of here, the better," was said more than once, and when the last log went through the port-hole, we gave three cheers so loud the captain (who was ashore at the time) said the whole town heard it.

Then the carpenter said to me: "George, my boy, get the pot boiling while I fasten the porthole up ready for caulking."

Now that the time left at Sierra Leone was short, our spirits rose and it was great fun to see the crew-boys pulling the palm trees off the ship. They leapt about and looked more like monkeys than men. The palm trees fell overboard, and floated on the water until the tide came in and pushed them ashore, where they were picked up by the crew-boys. Our captain came on board that night with six new sailors to replace the men who had died, and before the day dawned, we were working the windless for all we were worth, glad to get out of this 'hell' as the sailors called it. The heat dropped as we pulled away from

Shipwrecks and Bush Felling

Sierra Leone and when we got clear of the African coast, we basked in pure air.

"It's a relief to feel a cool breeze again," I said to the mate.

"Aye," he said, "but mark my words a storm is brewing. Good thing the old London is a good sea boat and can stand plenty of knocking about."

His words proved true. The seas became heavy and waves rose to awful heights, it was hard work and slow sailing, but we came to no harm.

This finishes the account of my first sea voyage. It took three months going, three months to load up, and three months coming home, so I arrived in London after a nine months voyage, a full-fledged sailor, or so I thought, still being a boy with a lot to learn. I was paid off at the shipping office with a six-pound cheque. Now I had money in my pocket there was no need to pinch a ride on the back of a cab. I felt quite the gentleman when I paid a cabby nine pence to drive me home in style.

When I got home, everyone was delighted to see me and I was delighted to see them, although it grieved me to find that my father was not as robust as I remembered him, as he had been very ill.

"I'm so glad to see you back safe and sound," said my mother. "I thought when you left, I would never see you again."

She also looked more worn than I remembered her, as in addition to worry over my father's illness there was money trouble.

But I put my cheque on the table and said, "Mother, we're alright now."

"Thanks be to the Lord," she said, and she wiped a tear

G.R. Meredith / W.E. Hamilton

from her eye, for the dear old soul needed it very much. My first cheque came in very useful and I was proud to know I had been a help to them in a time of need, and that (even more than the cab ride) made me feel a man.

───────────

Shipwrecks and Bush Felling

My Second Voyage

My mother made a cake to celebrate my safe return. Later that evening after dinner, my father drew me aside and said: "Stay home awhile, George, I'm feeling better but I have got behind in my orders."

"I can stay for three months, Dad," I said, "for there are no ships going to sea at this time, but then I will take the first ship that will have me."

"I had hoped you would have the sea out of your system after your first voyage," said Dad, disappointed. "Surely your dreadful experiences at Sierra Leone have put you off?"

And so they should have, but being young and optimistic, I hoped for better things with my next voyage. I knew I could get on a ship at any time as a first-class boy since Captain Fraser had given me a good character in my register ticket, which sailors always get after their first voyage. I kept my promise and helped my father in his business, although I still did not like blind making, I worked diligently to help my dear old Dad. About two weeks before the three months had passed, one of my old shipmates came to our home to see me, and of course our talk was all about the sea and sailors.

"I've just shipped in a vessel called The Commodore, George," he said, "and the captain of the Herald needs a strong lad at once and will give good wages."

When I heard this, I had to go and inquire about it, and felt pretty sure of getting the job since I had a 'good ticket' as sailors call it. When I got aboard the vessel, I was delighted to find she was a regular clipper, and I thought how proud I would be if I learned how to steer her, so when the captain came aboard that night, I said:

"Captain, I have sailed to Sierra Leone as a cabin boy and wish to join your ship if you will have me."

"Let me see your ticket," he said, looking me over.

I handed it to him confidently because it was a good one, and he read it carefully. "Well, boy, Captain Fraser gives you a good recommendation, and you look a strong lad, so I will ship you at one pound a month."

" That was good enough for me so I said, "thank you, Sir."

"But I'll warn you," he continued, "besides the ordinary sea work, there is heavy loading and unloading work to do in these fruit vessels. But if you do your duty, I will pay you off at the end of the voyage as an ordinary seaman."

This pleased me since it would give me a good start in my sea life, so I said, "thank you, Sir, I am not afraid of hard work."

We all set-to to get the Herald in good trim for the voyage. While we were busy, the owner came aboard with a long letter for Captain Lance, and shortly after the orders were given to "throw out large ropes and haul the ship to the end of the dock,

Shipwrecks and Bush Felling

ready for the river at daybreak."

That night we only got two hours sleep. I did not complain, though the rest of the crew nearly growled their heads off. At daylight we sailed up the river bound for St Michaels, one of the western islands for oranges, in what sailors called the green fruit trade.

When we got to Gravesend, the Skipper went ashore and got his clearance, then all sails were set and away we went. We had a headwind to the Downs, but to see the Herald lifting up to the wind, well, you couldn't wish for anything better in a sailor's life. She was a real beauty and fairly cut the wind in half as the sailor's term it. In three days we were in the English channel, scudding along in a regular bluster. After the low was over, we hung about the Bay of Biscay and the skipper seemed a bit troubled.

"If we get stuck in the Bay, it means a long passage," he said, looking glum.

"Why is that a problem?" I asked.

"It is a race to get the first fruit to London, for the first ship gets the bounty money of two and sixpence per box."

"Two and six, is a lot of money," I said.

"Aye," said the skipper, "what's more, it is divided among all hands. Even you, young nipper, will get some if we get the first fruit."

Then I too was troubled, for I wanted a share in the bounty as much as any other man there. But we had nothing to worry about. The Herald was too good a vessel to be held in the Bay. She lifted up to the wind and sailed through the channel like the good old boat she was. Away we went, right into the western ocean and very heavy seas, which she only laughed at.

G.R. Meredith / W.E. Hamilton

It was very rough coming home.

Shipwrecks and Bush Felling

After about three weeks sailing, we sighted our port, and when we got there, we let go the anchor a distance from the shore because the waterway was shallow-drafted.

"Here comes the fruit," said one of my shipmates called John, who had done this trip before. He pointed to several large barges heading towards us.

"Hoist the flats and get ready to receive the fruit," commanded the captain, who had also seen them.

Then we lowered flat-bottomed boats into the water.

"When they get here, transfer the load as quickly as possible," said the captain, "for loading in an open roadstead it not ideal, we have the whole of the Western Sea to contend with, should the weather turn bad."

I did not know what a roadstead was and there was no time to ask as by now the barges had come alongside us. I found out later that a roadstead was a body of water sheltered from rip currents, spring tides or ocean swells. As the captain said, it was not an ideal way to load a ship, but as there was no harbour in that area, we had no other choice. To make matters worse, the only way to get a full cargo of fruit was to throw overboard twenty tons of sand ballast to make room for twenty tons of fruit.

"I don't like this," said John, looking at the gathering clouds. "This is a risky business, if the weather turns bad, we could be blown out to sea without our ballast."

But once again God's hand was watching over me. There were only two or three boats in the roadstead, so we were able to get all the boats alongside us which greatly aided the speed of transfer. Then over the side went the ballast and in came the fruit.

G.R. Meredith / W.E. Hamilton

Now I remembered the captains warning of heavy work, and he had not exaggerated at all. It was hard slog for about ten days. While we were getting our cargo, another clipper called The Black Cat came alongside. The Black Cat had broken every record in the fruit trade, and as both vessels were leaving at the same time, the captains signaled to one another.

"I am for the first fruit in London," shouted the captain of The Black Cat.

"Don't be too sure of that," replied our skipper.

Away we went with every stitch of canvas we could carry. And it was a sight worth seeing, these two vessels travelling. The Black Cat kept us astir of her for the first two days and then we had headwinds. Our skipper rubbed his hands at the wheel and said, "now Mr. Cat I've got you."

And so we had. The Herald lifted to the wind, showed her tail to the old Cat and away we went. We did not see her again until she got to the London docks. By then her main boom was gone and her mainsail all in ribbons, as she was caught in a gale off the Sicily Island near Land's End England. So, we beat her by six days and got our bounty money, which (added to our wages) made a good cheque. The work was hard but I did not mind, as the money was good and I was strong and healthy. After discharging our cargo and trimming up our vessel, we were ready for another voyage to the same port. No bounty this time, however, as it was only given for the first cargo of fruit.

Shipwrecks and Bush Felling

Out to Sea Again

Two of the crew left the Herald and joined a larger vessel, but I stuck to the old ship and made the second voyage. This time I had some idea of what to expect. But a sea voyage always has an element of uncertainty for that is the nature of the sea. The trip out was uneventful and loading the fruit went well. Had it very rough coming home, however. Heavy seas in the Atlantic Ocean, carried away all our upper gear. Altogether it was a terrible voyage and much damage was done to some boxes of oranges. We were a sorry sight when we limped into the Downes with what the sailors call bare poles. At the Downes the tug boat fastened on to us and away we went to Gravesend, where we let go our anchor and awaited orders.

"Clear up as best you can," said the captain, "though I fear there is little we can do to make the ship look better."

When the owners came from London, they were amazed to see the wreck of the old Herald, and when they saw the damage to the cargo, spoke some strong words to the skipper.

But Captain Lance was too good for them.

"You should be thankful I got this vessel home as good as it is," he said. "If it were not for my noble crew, there would be nothing left to find fault with."

He got his logbook and read it to them which made them see things in a different light. I heard no more of the conversation as I went into the cabin to talk things over with the others. But the mate told us to go to bed.

"For I know you are in much need of rest," he said. "I will keep watch in the meantime."

You may be sure we did not need telling twice, for we were all dead beat, and I for one made up for the lost time and slept soundly. At eight bells the mate came to rouse me and I was up on deck before the mate was in his cabin. About three hours later, the mate came back on deck.

"Now clear up a bit," he said, "square the rigging as much as you can."

Here is where I learned a lot of seamanship, such as splicing ropes, etc. While we were working, the merchant to whom the cargo belonged came on board, and up went the hatches and out came the cargo of oranges. We all looked pretty blue expecting the fruit to be very damaged. Nevertheless, we eagerly prized the lids off the boxes, anxious to see what condition the oranges were in. The boxes when they landed on the deck looked bad, but on closer investigation, they were better than we thought.

"I think the fruit will be alright," said the merchant smiling.

That was good news for us all. Once the merchant had gone, the captain examined the damaged fruit further. He was pleased to find the cargo not as bad as he expected, and showed his pleasure by treating us. He called the mate over and said

Shipwrecks and Bush Felling

something to him. Then the mate called out in a loud voice:

"Splice the main brace boys."

At this, we all rushed around the mate like a lot of schoolboys and had a glass of old rum.

After that we had to work hard getting the cargo ashore, but we did not mind as the captain had treated us. In the end, of all the boxes sent ashore at Gravesend, only twenty boxes of fruit were damaged, and we heard later, they sold at the auction for as much as the good ones. But the ship did not fare as well as the oranges.

"Do you think the old Herald will sail again?" I asked Captain Lance.

"No George," said the captain, "I don't think we shall be shipmates on the old boat again, and as for the hull, it's shot."

"I am sad to hear that," I said. For unlike the captains of the large vessels, Captain Lance was a kind man, just as many of the captains of the smaller vessels were. Those captains depended more on their crew, and if they got a good crew, nothing was too good for them.

"As am I," said the captain, looking about the shattered ship. "You gave the best food," I said.

"And plenty of hard work," he smiled.

"Yes, plenty of hard work," I laughed.

"The Commodore is looking for more crew, George. You'd do well to apply to the captain for a place on her."

I thanked him for his advice and the next day I went on board the Commodore to see the captain, and came away more than satisfied. He promised to send me word when he was ready to sail. So, after bidding him goodbye, I took a cab to my home.

G.R. Meredith / W.E. Hamilton

A Secret Cargo

As you can imagine my family were very pleased to see me when I got home. Thomas and little Charles had grown since I saw them last, as is the usual way of children. After being home for about ten days I got a letter to say the Commodore would be sailing in a week's time, and I was to be in the shipping office two days before we sailed.

So, I packed up for another voyage and was very pleased to get on a boat where I was shipped as first class ordinary seaman; which is next to being an able seaman. I got aboard and did my days' work, and gained as much information as I could as to where we were bound, before going ashore that night. Then I went to play and had a good flair up, knowing that it was to be my last night ashore for some time.

Next day we commenced clearing up and fixed all the gear so it was ready for sea. Later that day we shifted the ship to the outer end of the dock to take in cargo. We loaded two holds with foodstuffs, and clothing for soldiers, but nothing went into the main holds, which was very strange. When we were

Shipwrecks and Bush Felling

finished, the tug boat got hold of us and away we went as far as Gravesend where we had to anchor as the tide was too strong. While we waited, we all went down below.

"This is a smart yacht," I said.

"Aye, it is, but where is it bound for, that is what I'd like to know?" said one fellow.

"It's all very secretive" said another.

"Some war, by the look of our cargo," I said.

Great was the speculation between us over this matter; some thought one place and others thought another. By and by we talked ourselves to sleep and knew no more until daybreak.

We were up at dawn and the old tug was puffing at our bows as the sun peeped above the horizon, ready to get hold of us as soon as the anchor was cleared off the ground.

"Open the main hatch, men," said the mate, "we have more cargo to come aboard."

We exchanged glances among ourselves, but said nothing as two large boats came alongside us. When we saw that two officers (wearing brass buttons) accompanied the boats, we all wondered what next? Then up came a lot of brass-bound boxes and the officers with brass buttons stowed them carefully below. When all was finished, they stayed on deck until we fixed and battened the hatches down. Then one of them put a seal on the hatches as big as a teacup while the other went to the captain to sign for the boxes.

"Captain Nance, I need your signature," said the officer.

"Is it as was agreed?" said Captain Nance.

"Yes, five hundred pounds paid to the shipowner for the safe delivery of the boxes, with a forfeit of four hundred pounds if anything goes wrong with them."

"Where is my part of the deal?" said Captain Nance, skimming the document.

"Down here," said the officer, stabbing his finger on the paper.

"Ah, here it is," said the captain, "once the boxes are delivered, the five hundred pounds will be split fifty-fifty between the captain and the shipowner."

"That's a nice little nest egg for you, Captain," smiled the officer.

"Provided God is with us and nothing goes amiss," said the captain, signing with a shaky hand. "I share in the profit if we are successful, but I also share in the loss if things go amuck. Two hundred pounds is a lot to lose and the sea is capricious."

"It is indeed," nodded the officer, taking the paper from the captain and folding it up. "Best of luck."

Of course, I knew nothing of this agreement at the time, I only learnt of it later. All I knew then was that the officer was with the captain a long time. Eventually they finished talking. I expected the officers to get back into their boats, but surprisingly they did not leave.

"Call all hands on deck," said the captain to the mate.

When we were all assembled before him, he addressed us solemnly.

"We have very valuable cargo aboard and I shall depend on you men as a trusty crew to do your duty to me and my mate."

Then the young sailor who was acting as our spokesman replied:

"Yes captain, you can depend upon us doing our duty while the Commodore is above water." And we all gave three hearty cheers to show our loyalty.

Shipwrecks and Bush Felling

"Hurry up and clear the decks, George," said the captain, looking well pleased, "once that is done, we will splice the main brace."

You may be sure we were very happy when we heard this. After having our grog, we cleaned up again before supper and went to bed.

We did some swift travelling.

G.R. Meredith / W.E. Hamilton

The mud pilot hailed me during my watch at four the next morning.

"Anyone aboard?" he called.

"Yes," I said, "what do you want?"

"I am the pilot, lower the gangway ladder down."

So over went the ladder and up came the pilot. I called up the mate and said:

"The pilot is aboard."

"All hands on deck," called the mate.

Then everyone scrambled on deck and the pilot took charge of the vessel until we got to Deal. As soon as the anchor cleared the ground, the mate called me aft to take the wheel and then the pilot said:

"Do you see that point on the lee of the bow, George?"

"Yes, Sir."

"Keep the nose fair at it until further orders, don't look anywhere else."

"Yes, Sir."

I felt quite the man as I took the wheel for although I had been on several voyages by now, I was still young in years. I locked my eyes on the point as the pilot instructed and headed straight for it. Having a good tide and plenty of sea room, all went well and the next day we were at Deal, where the pilot left us, along with the brass-button-officers and Mrs. Nance the captain's wife.

Once they were gone, the captain called us together.

"Men, we are bound under sealed orders to go to Gibraltar and after that Messina, a port in the Mediterranean where we can get cargo. Now lads, do what lies before you. But no main brace this time, for I wish you to have clear heads until you are

Shipwrecks and Bush Felling

sure of the vessel and know what she can do."

We got on with our work and the hand of God was with us. The weather was good and (as everything was in our favour) the Commodore did some swift travelling until we got to the mouth of the channel where the wind chopped around in our teeth. It was my shift and Captain Nance seeing me at the wheel, asked:

"What do you think of her George?"

"Well Captain," I replied, "she beats our old boat in the beam but this headwind will try her." The captain nodded. "She is a good steering boat, take her up to the wind to see what she can do."

So, I took her up to the wind, but I found she couldn't hold her own with a headwind as the other boat could.

"We'll have to keep on tacking in the channel, in what the sailors call the 'long and short,' George," said the captain.

"Why is it called that?" I asked.

"The short leg keeps us off the shore and the long leg lets us make headway," said the captain. "You'll find sailing like this is hard work."

He was right. We had a week's hard labour at this game before we got fine weather with the wind in the beam. Once we had that, she travelled well until we got near the gulf of Gibraltar and another bluster came. We tried to tackle the Gulf but it was no go, so we tried to lay to, but again no go. The ship would not lie stationary with her bow to the wind. This is the only vessel I have sailed in all the time I was at sea that would not lay to with fore-topmast but the old Commodore being stubborn, would not have it any price. Accordingly, we had to come the long leg and short leg again which made a lot of work for me. You may be sure we had to get the skipper to splice the main brace pretty often to cheer us up a little. We had about ten days at this game until finally we got another fair wind and made for the gulf of Gibraltar. We got about halfway up when down came the Government tug boat, fastened on to us and away we went full sail with the anchor in readiness.

"We're really coming into the harbour in style," said a shipmate, as a boat came alongside us.

And he was quite right. I had never been on a voyage where we were met with such official ceremony. Grim looking officers and soldiers came on board and stood on guard while we unbuttoned the hatch. And you may be sure they took good care to see that their large seal was not tampered with. The officers, noting the safe delivery of the boxes, left the cargo below and replaced the hatches. For the rest of the time the boxes remained on the ship, four soldiers were posted on guard to watch over them.

"What do you think is in the boxes?" we wondered quietly among ourselves.

"It must be something of great value," I said, "because there is such a fuss being made."

Next day a large [1]lighter came alongside for the boxes.

"George, go down into the hatchway and sling up the boxes," said the captain.

I scurried down below and two of the soldiers came after me and stood over me as I slung the boxes up.

I never found out what those boxes contained, but whatever it was, the soldiers thought they were important enough to stay watching me until the very last box was out of our ship and

---

1   Flat-bottomed boat.

Shipwrecks and Bush Felling

stowed safely in their lighter. Once that was done, the captain came to one of the soldiers to sign a paper, and you may be sure he was relieved when the soldier signed the receipt for the safe delivery of the boxes.

"Cover the hatches, men," he said, and when we had done that, he gave the welcome command to "splice the main brace."

"I'm glad that job is done," I said, voicing the general thought as I drank my rum. "I didn't like all that humbug."

My shipmates growled their agreement.

"Now we have nothing to do other than look after the rest of the cargo in the usual way," said the mate.

He could not have been more wrong for our strange adventures were not yet over.

G.R. Meredith / W.E. Hamilton

A Princess and a Sea Chase

We were all relieved when the lighter carrying the soldiers and officers disappeared from sight.

With all the humbug I had forgotten the soldier's clothing and foodstuff until two more lighters pulled alongside us.

"Now that is all over and done with, men," said the mate, "time to discharge the rest of the cargo."

So up went the hatches and out came the cargo, one hatch for the light goods and the other for the heavier, and plenty of hard work for all hands. The skipper and mate worked with us until we got down to the ballast in the hold.

"I'm going ashore to look around for more ballast," said the skipper to the mate. "I'll leave half the crew with you on the boat and the other half can have a holiday."

I stayed on the ship with the mate while some of the others went ashore. They were away longer than we expected.

"I had terrible trouble finding ballast," the skipper told the

Shipwrecks and Bush Felling

mate. "There was not a rock or bag of sand to be had."

"What are we going to do?" said the mate. "We will bobble about like a cork on the sea without more ballast."

"I managed to get a cargo bound for the other side of the rock. Hopefully, I will find more ballast there," said the skipper. "The lighter will be here any minute."

And sure enough, he had hardly finished speaking when it arrived. So once again it was up with the hatches and in with the cargo. While we were working, the mail boat came in.

"A letter from the owner," said the skipper, slitting the letter open.

"What does he have to say?" said the mate.

"There is a cargo of sulphur at Messina for us if we can not get cargo anywhere else," said the skipper, smiling. "Tell the men when they have finished loading to get ready for the sea."

So, in obedience to the mate's command, we set off and were soon around the Rock of Gibraltar and into the Mediterranean, where a fair wind blew us right into the harbour. While we were discharging the cargo, the skipper looked about for ballast and this time was successful. We loaded in the ballast, and then we were off to Messina for the load of sulphur. The trip to Messina was one of the few patches of this journey that was uneventful, for once we got there, things got strange again. We docked at Messina and were loading the sulphur when there was a rebellion of some sort.

"I don't like this," said the skipper, looking at the soldiers flooding into the area. The words were hardly out of his mouth when we heard a shot fired. "We'd best get out of here quick."

We hastily loaded the last of the sulphur, shut the hatches and got ready to go down the harbour. But before we could get clear of the dock, the British Consul and twelve big fellows came running down the wharf; with them was a young princess and a lot of boxes.

"Wait," shouted the British Consul rushing aboard. "I will pay you a hundred and fifty pounds to take us with you."

"You don't even know where we are going," said the skipper.

"It doesn't matter," said the British Consul, "anywhere is fine so long as we are under the British flag and you hurry."

As the quarrel was not ours, and a hundred and fifty pounds was a lot of money, the bargain was struck. And not a moment too soon, for we were hardly clear of the wharf when a mob came to seize our passengers.

"Hurry, men," shouted the mate.

So, while the British Consul hustled the princess into the cabin, and the soldiers stood at the ready, we made the old Commodore do her best. We were almost out of the Gulf when we saw a large vessel coming after us.

"Run up every sail," shouted the mate. "They are after us!"

We did not need to be told twice. We clapped on all sails and soon lost it. There was no sign of our pursuers by the time we got to the rock. There we put the princess and the men all safely on shore, and the skipper received his reward.

The talk, as we loaded a cargo of raisins on top of our load of sulphur, all revolved around the mysterious princess.

"I reckon she was Princess Luisa Fernanda," said Arnie, who was the best read of us all. "The British and the French are fighting over who she and her sister Queen Isabella will marry."

"Could be," nodded Harry, "the vessel that came after us

Shipwrecks and Bush Felling

was French."

"I'm getting sick of all this humbug and mysterious boxes," I said.

"Those boxes would have been the least of our troubles if the French had caught us," said Arnie, "for sure they would have hung the lot of us."

The idea sent shivers down our spines and made us homesick for dear old England. We finished loading the raisins in record time, for we were keen to get shot of the place and head for home. We got a fair wind through the strait of Gibraltar and had fine weather all the passage back.

When we docked in London, the captain got word of the birth of a son.

"That explains why Mrs. Nance did not come with us this time," said Arnie, as we drank to the health of the mother and baby.

By the time we had all the cargo ashore I was very glad to be finished up.

"I'm not signing on again," I said to Harry, "there is too much work attached to these small boats."

"What are you thinking to do instead, George?"

"Now I am an Able Seaman and have the best registered tickets from my skippers, I have made up my mind to tackle a larger ship."

"Well, good luck to you," said Harry, shaking my hand as we departed.

I went to the Tower Hill shipping office to find another ship. You would think after my last voyage I would have stayed clear of any place at war. But as youth is optimistic and I was determined not to sail on another small boat, I

G.R. Meredith / W.E. Hamilton

shipped in the barque called the Chatham. The Chatham was hired by the government to carry troops to the West Indies. My optimism was rewarded with a trip that was so uneventful it is not worth telling about. We called at Barbados and landed fifty-four soldiers, before taking on condemned guns and rifles and two hundred invalid soldiers, who we took straight to the government docks in London. This ended for me a nine months voyage of varied happiness.

Shipwrecks and Bush Felling

Shipwreck

When I got home, my family were delighted to see me.

"How long are you staying, George?" asked my father.

"I've shipped in a barque bound for Bristol that leaves in a week's time," I said, glad to have it all arranged, for I did not want him to ask me to help with the blinds again.

"You've grown and you look well," said my mother.

"Did you have any adventures?" asked Thomas.

"I certainly did," I said, taking the cup of tea Mum handed me. "We rescued a princess and got chased by a ship."

"Now, now, George, don't tell sailor's tall tales to your little brothers," said my mother. "They will believe everything you say."

"But it is perfectly true, Mum, we did rescue a princess. We were never told her name but one of my shipmates thought she was Queen Isabella of Spain's younger sister."

"Fancy that," said Dad.

"Oh Georgie, I hope you weren't in any danger?" said Mum, turning pale.

G.R. Meredith / W.E. Hamilton

"Jim says they would have hung the lot of us if they caught us," I said proudly, "but we were too fast for them."

"Did you see soldiers," asked Charles, fingering his toy soldier.

"Lots of them, Charly. "We took troops to the West Indies on my next ship and bought back the wounded."

"Were many wounded?" asked Thomas.

"Too many," I said shuddering, "the ship was like a floating hospital.

All too soon the week was up. I went to the London docks and boarded the barque. Unlike my other jobs I was paid my wages ahead of time, which turned out to be a good thing. Moreover, wheat seemed a safe and uncomplicated cargo. But as it happened, we had more trouble with the wheat than the princess, secret boxes, and soldiers, all rolled together. Our trouble started in the Bristol Channel near the Newport lighthouse.

"Man the pumps," yelled the mate, "we've sprung a leak."

We set-to, but it was no use the water kept coming in. And all the time we were pumping we could see the wheat growing as it soaked up the water.

"This blasted wheat will be the end of the ship," said the captain to the mate, "turn the flag upside down, and pray the lighthouse will see our distress, for the rate the wheat is swelling we can't last much longer."

Alas, the captain was right, nevertheless, we struggled on ever mindful of our growing cargo. By the time the wheat had grown to such a size there was no room for us below, we saw a lighter coming towards us. The West Esk lighthouse keeper had seen our Union Jack upside down and was coming to our

Shipwrecks and Bush Felling

rescue. We scrambled onto the lighter just in time, as with a loud crack our ship broke clean in half and sank below the water.

We were taken to the lighthouse and by the time we got there we were weary and hungry. We had a [2]shakedown on the hard stone floor but there was nothing to fill our rumbling bellies with. The lighthouse keeper, who was a hospitable man, was distressed that he was not able to offer us refreshments.

"I would like to give you and your men something to eat, Captain," he said looking worried, "but I am required to keep a certain amount of food in stock in case of bad weather, for it is uncertain when a boat can deliver food."

But once again God's hand was upon me, the Humane Society sent a little steamboat with stores for the keeper the very next day. We were very pleased to see her as she puffed towards us, for if she had not come, we might have been there for weeks and starved. So, we arrived at Bristol by steamboat instead of our fine ship. It could have been a difficult situation, but as we had received our payment before leaving, we were alright. We found a boarding house and 'let go our anchor' at The Sailors Rest until we found another ship to take us home.

---

[2]   Makeshift bed.

G.R. Meredith / W.E. Hamilton

Disaster

After I had been home for ten days, I decided it was time to return to the London docks to find work.

"Why don't you stay here until after Christmas," said my mother, "it is scarcely more than a week away."

But I was restless and keen to go, so I wished them a Merry Christmas and bid them goodbye.

"Write and let us know what ship you are on," said Dad hugging me.

"I will," I promised.

When I got to London, I shipped in a rig called the Lady Grant. She was bound for New Orleans with railway iron. Because I had not forgotten my promise to my father, I sent him word that I was sailing on the Lady Grant. The letter had scarcely gone when fate stepped in and I missed my passage on her. At the time I was much upset, for it never occurred to me I might miss her.

"Such a thing has never happened to me before," I lamented

Shipwrecks and Bush Felling

to the man in the shipping office.

"Don't worry," he said, "The Lady West of Newport is going in that direction and the captain is looking for crew."

Here is where I now see God's hand upon me. I shipped in The Lady West, not the Lady Grant; and lucky I did. For the Lady Grant foundered in the Bay of Biscay, got lost and never came out again. All hands went down with her. When the news hit the London papers, my dear old Dad thought I was among the dead.

But instead, I was on the Lady of the West. She was a large barque carrying two thousand tons of railway iron to New Orleans. Of greater interest to me than the cargo, however, was the dog that sailed aboard her. Although it was not uncommon to have animals on ships, mostly they were chickens or goats, for their eggs and milk made a welcome addition to our diet. I was delighted by this discovery as I was fond of dogs and old Carlo and I quickly became firm friends.

"He's a fine dog," I said, scratching behind his ears.

Nobody answered because at that moment the butcher came up the gangplank carrying a quarter of a bullock.

"Did you see all that meat go into the galley?" said one of my new shipmates called Robert.

"I overheard the captain tell the cook we were to have extra fare and sea pie because it is the festive season," piped up the cabin boy.

We were very much looking forward to this treat, and we thought of it as we set off. But alas, we did not get our dinner after all, for bad weather set in. Instead of roast meat and sea pie, all we got was a bad knocking about near the Bay of Biscay. We thought we would be driven into the bay and never come out, but at eight bells one night, there was a change of wind.

"Throw up every stitch of canvas," shouted the mate, wishing to take advantage of the wind to get a grand start.

"Now we shall do some tall travelling," said Robert in satisfaction, "we'll show our tails to this wicked old bay."

But our jubilation was cut short. The wind changed and the sea became mountainous. We tried to turn the ship around but it was impossible because of the heavy sea, so instead, we sailed onward as it was the safest way in the dreadful conditions. At length (to our relief) we sailed out of the storm and the weather improved greatly. It continued to be good and our spirits rose as we looked forward to a merry time. But four days before Christmas the weather turned, and once again we were disappointed. The wind, blowing seventy miles an hour through the rigging, sounded like an unearthly scream. And the waves were so high we found it necessary to pump the vessel out every dog watch[3] all through the night.

Then to add to our peril, the bilge pump stopped working. The carpenter came along and said: "What are you chaps doing? The water needs pumping out."

"She ought to have been sucked dry half an hour ago," I said.

"Well, she's not. When I used the sounding rod, I found we've four foot of water in the hold."

"Hey, the pump is not sucking and no water's coming out," I shouted to the second mate.

The second mate went down into the hold with the captain to see what was wrong.

"There's the problem," said the second mate, pointing to a

---

3   A half shift of two hours.

Shipwrecks and Bush Felling

lot of loose iron sliding about.

The words were scarcely out of his mouth when they heard a rush of water.

"Watch out," cried the captain, but it was too late.

The heavy water picked up the second mate and dashed him amongst a lot of loose bars of iron. He was killed instantly. The captain came out of the hold, grey-faced and alone.

"All hands to the pump," he shouted.

So, we pumped for all we were worth.

That Christmas was the worst Christmas of my life. We never did get to eat the roast beef and sea pie we were so looking forward to, for we spent it manning the pumps. Then about five o'clock that evening, disaster struck. We found we were still taking water on despite two powerful pumps. The carpenter used his sounding rod and found six-foot of water in the hold.

Once again, the captain went down to investigate the problem, this time with the carpenter.

"There's the trouble," said the carpenter, turning pale, "one of the bars has gone through her bottom.

Meanwhile, we kept pumping, right up until the moment the poor old Lady West started going down to Davy Jones' Locker. By the time the captain and the carpenter came back, the end was near; the old Lady had begun to heel over on her beam ends.

"She's sinking. Clear away the boats and then every man for himself," came the orders.

At this I rushed into the galley and grabbed half a bag of spuds and a tub of biscuits. Some oilskin coats were hanging by the door so I took them too, thinking we might be able to make good use of them later on.

"Help me with the longboat, George," shouted the carpenter, dumping four kegs into it as he swung the [4]davits out.

I threw my supplies into the boat and we started to lower it over the side, but as we did, the ship gave a terrible roll and our boat went with her. I thought for a moment that the boat and I were going to get caught under her, but by some miracle we escaped, clearing the side of the ship by a small margin. As it was likely the old Lady would never right herself again, I jumped into the boat and bet her away from the doomed vessel. While I was doing this, the carpenter went to the cabin for the captain and his wife. Then together they slithered down the slippery deck and I helped them into the boat. I heard barking and turning my head saw old Carlo standing at the side of the ship.

"Come on Carlo," I called. Without hesitation, he jumped overboard and swam to the boat and I hauled him over the side.

There were four lifeboats in all; three smaller boats and one longboat. We, with seventeen aboard the longboat, had to be very careful to keep the boat head on to the sea, otherwise we ran the risk of being swamped broadside and capsizing. But it was not so with the other boats. They could face the sea any which way. While these boats were getting clear of the davits some of the men went into the cabin and salvaged two kegs of wine that the captain had for his wife. They also got the sailing gear belonging to the boat. Meanwhile, the vessel was sinking fast by the bows, so we had no time to lose, for we knew if the ship went down while we were alongside, she would take us all with her.

---

4   Small cranes the lifeboats are attached to.

Shipwrecks and Bush Felling

Seventeen were aboard the longboat.

"Hurry up," shouted the captain, "get into the lifeboats before it's too late."

Then suddenly the Lady West stopped rolling and sat on the water like a duck.

Now everyone who was not already in a boat hastened into one. And not a moment too soon. For a rolling sea came at the poor old Lady's stern, threw her bows underwater, and she went down nose-first. We were not more than twenty chains from her when she made her final plunge, going down straight on end. We watched her as she disappeared and could see her name right up to the end, for her stern went last. We felt like we had witnessed the death of a friend and we sat in silence for a few moments looking at the empty place where she had been a few minutes ago. Then suddenly someone gave a shout.

"Look, she's coming up again."

And sure enough, she was, but not in a way that was helpful to us. She had broken clean in half and came up in two pieces. Then because of the danger of being dashed against the wreck, the first mate shouted:

"Move away."

So, we moved as far away from her as we could. And that was the last I saw of the Lady West.

Shipwrecks and Bush Felling

Adrift at Sea

A place was made for the captain's wife in the stern of the boat, and the dog got under my seat and never moved from me. Dear old Carlo, if we were all as faithful to one another as he was, how much happier we could all be.

Nearby casts of water floated on the sea. Guthrie, an old seaman of twenty years handed me an oar and said:

"See if you can get a cask, George."

But the sea was too much for us, and fearing that the casks might rush about and go right through the boat, we gave up and let them float away.

Then the two boats that had secured a sail went before the wind and swiftly departed. The other boat kept beside us until the next day, when we lost sight of it, and we heard afterwards that they got on better than we did.

The captain, setting us on a certain course, said:

"Take up the oars and pull hard, men, we are only about a hundred miles from the French coast and might meet a French fishing vessel if we are lucky."

For the first two days we stuck to our course and made as much headway as we could, but she was a heavy boat made to carry eight to ten tons. By the fourth day we were weak and in need of water and, consequently, made little headway with our boat. So, the captain gave us a ration of wine.

"Here you are, men," he said, giving us each a small cup of wine and half a biscuit. "This will help a little."

"Only a very little," growled Guthrie.

Then some of the men got quite noisy and the mate had to call them to order.

"That's enough of that," he said. "Who has a knife?"

We pulled them out and showed them to him. He chose the best one and put it under the seat where the captain's wife sat, for he knew that was the safest place for it.

"Now throw your knives overboard," he commanded.

So, every knife (except for the one the captain's wife guarded) went into the sea.

That night came a strong wind and a heavy sea which was miserable. But following that came some blessed rain which cheered us all up again. I was very glad I had thought to grab the oilskins from the galley, for we spread the coats across the boat and caught some much-needed water. The mate then emptied half the wine overboard and filled up the kegs with water. That blessed mixture did cheer us and gladden our hearts, but further trouble was to come, for the old boat shipped the sea over the stern, and all our biscuits were soaked with salt water making them impossible to eat without going mad with thirst. But the wine and water kept us going.

"Cheer up men, we might see a ship today," said the mate.

Shipwrecks and Bush Felling

We hoped fervently he was right, but no such luck.

The lookout in the bows was so anxious he was ever crying out, "sail oh," when there was nothing more than a large seagull floating on the top of the sea. Guthrie had the misfortune to be seated near the biscuits. In his hunger he grabbed more than his ration and suffered for his sins by going mad for liquid.

"Watch out," I shouted, as he tackled one of the men, making for his nose.

A man on either side of him held him down, but when the mate chucked the rest of the biscuits overboard, this poor fellow got so bad he threw his restrainers off and tried to tackle the mate. In the tussle that followed, he went overboard and took a lot of drowning before we lost sight of him. It was a sad sight to see.

I was stuck fast to my seat being so long cramped up in the same position. My poor Carlos, with his head between my knees, kept looking up to me for help, but I could not do anything. The seas continued very rough but the good old boat faced them boldly. We had to keep her head to sea for safety.

Another day passed, but no luck again. Our lookout called, "sail oh," again.

"Where, where?"

We all scanned the horizon eagerly. But once more it was a floating gull on top of a high sea. They certainly looked like small vessels to an eager watcher. When we knew it was another false alarm, we collapsed on our oars and could not row anymore. The mate then gave us another drink and two potatoes each, and I think the potatoes bucked me up more than the wine.

G.R. Meredith / W.E. Hamilton

The Darkest Hour

We had been lost at sea for five days when the mate said to me:

"Now George, we must have the dog and since he is with you, you can manage him better than any of us, I have the knife ready for you."

I was appalled by his words.

"I cannot kill old Carlo, I would sooner be killed myself," I said with passion.

"You must be mad to talk like that," said the mate. "If we don't see a sail soon, we might have to cast lots for ourselves yet, and you may be the first on the list."

"I don't care if I live or die," I said, "I cannot kill old Carlo."

The mate must not have been keen on the idea himself, for he did not press me to do the horrible deed.

By the sixth morning I felt even if I lived to tell of this ordeal, I would be crippled all my life. Like the others, I couldn't rise from my seat. By then we were all rolled up like

Shipwrecks and Bush Felling

a ball and couldn't stand to use the oars. In the dawn light, the mate pulled in his oar and handed me the knife.

"Come now, George, the deed must be done."

But I refused to kill the dog.

"I would rather die myself. If you must have Carlo, you must kill him yourself for I cannot." Then the mate got angry and seized the dog from the back of my seat and had the knife across his throat.

Never will I forget the hideous moment.

My dear old Carlo was soon cut up and his blood divided amongst them. I could not eat any, but begged the mate to give me a potato instead. After the dog was cut up in small pieces, it was placed in the bottom of the boat, free for all to help themselves when they felt that raving thirst.

"Now men, if we do not see a sailboat by tomorrow," said the mate, later that dreadful day, "we must cast lots, for by doing so we may leave some to tell the tale of our adventure."

I was glad to take my chance, for I was getting mad for a drink and my heart was grieved to think I was eating the flesh of my much-loved dog. And even all these years later, I am so overcome as I relate this awful experience, I wish I had not mentioned that terrible week. And yet despite this, I see now that God's hand was with me, though I did not know God then, as I do now.

By nightfall there was still no sign of a sail. The lookout man had nothing to say as he had slumped into despair. On the seventh day it was fine and clear and a small hope of rescue rekindled, but midday came and still no sail. Every minute I dreaded the mate would carry out his threat of casting lots, for today was the day he said it must be done. But he was as reluctant as the rest of us. We only had twenty potatoes left and parts of my old Carlo in the bottom of the boat, but it was enough to buy us another day.

"If we do not see a sail today, we will cast lots tomorrow morning," said the mate, putting off the unthinkable deed.

Our lookout man still stuck to his post, for he seemed to cheer up a bit even without a ration of wine. For although the wine was still with us, we were not allowed any for fear of mutiny or murder, as some of the men were prepared to do anything to get water or blood. The captain had lapsed into hopelessness; watching his wife waste away was too much for him. The mate, however, was a courageous man and ruled us with a rod of iron. It was an awful sight to see us next to madness for the want of water. We didn't miss the food so much but the constant cry was for water. I felt that I would gladly have been a slave for the rest of my life for a cup of cold water.

At seven o'clock on the seventh day, the lookout startled us by crying out:

"Sail oh, by God."

Then he dropped down on the bow of the boat and never moved again. We all thought he had fainted from weakness and excitement and took no notice of him, for the ship on our weather bow commanded our full attention.

"Pull for your life, boys," cried the mate, "I fear there is no sign of them seeing us!"

But the captain got his wife's red petticoat, and with his belt secured it to an oar and hoisted it as a signal. That red petticoat saved our lives. Not more than half an hour later, we saw the vessel's back and topsail. We tried to give three

Shipwrecks and Bush Felling

cheers, but we were so weak and overcome, we were unable to produce a sound. The mate kept waving our flag for dear life while I steadied the bottom of the oar as best I could. When the vessel saw the signal, she bore down on us, while we expended all our remaining strength to meet her. When she got close to our lee side, her crew threw out a rope to make fast our boat. We were all too exhausted to help ourselves, so the captain of the vessel got ready to hoist us aboard with a big tackle. But we all cried:

"Take the captain and his wife first."

So, a ballast basket was sent down for them.

Once the captain and his wife were on board, the rest of us went up one by one. Finally, only the lookout man remained in the bottom of the boat, still lying in the position he fell. Some of us went down to rouse him. But when we got to him, we found that he was dead and another basket had to be sent down for him. It was a grieving sight to see his body as it rolled out of the basket and onto the deck.

Then the only thing we had eyes for was the cask of water on the deck nearby, and we crawled towards it on our hands and knees.

"Get back," commanded the mate of the vessel, sitting on top of the cask. "You shall all have your share of water." Then he gave each one of us a pannikin of water and a biscuit.

Never before or after has water tasted so good. Once we had eaten and drunk, we crawled into some coils of rope and slept soundly until morning.

G.R. Meredith / W.E. Hamilton

Homeward Bound

Our position, when the schooner Fanny of Slacome rescued us, was somewhere on the south-west coast of England. She was bound for St Michaels for oranges. Her mate was a good sort, but I didn't think much of the captain.

At eight bells next morning, the mate came to us and gave us more water and biscuits.

"Try to crawl to the main hatch by eleven o'clock," he said, "and we will bury your shipmate." The burial service was read by our captain. This was the second soul overboard, leaving now fifteen out of the seventeen that started out in the longboat.

The Fanny crew were very kind to us. After the funeral they carried us like babies and made us comfortable in the hold with blankets. Then after giving us more biscuits and water, we again slept and awoke feeling refreshed. Because of the attention of the crew, we picked up wonderfully and soon got quite strong again. We decided to go to St Michaels where the English Consul would send us home in the first vessel going

Shipwrecks and Bush Felling

that way.

Meanwhile, our old boat (tied to the schooner with a very strong rope) was tearing at the stern, for the captain of the Fanny was keen to get her to St Michael's as he would get bounty money for her. But alas, we ran into a heavy gale and after a few days of rough seas, she copped a huge wave, snapped the rope and sunk. That was the end of the good old boat that had ferried us through danger and suffering and saved our lives. And that was not the end of our bad luck. We never got to St Michael's because the Fanny got bad winds and was driven very much out of her course. Fortunately, however, we were blown into the path of homeward-bound vessels. About four days later, we sighted a brig close by so we hailed her.

"Ahoy, Captain, this is the Captain of the Fanny Slacome. We have a wrecked crew on board and we were getting short of water."

"This is the Captain of the Esther of Liverpool bound for Falmouth for orders," came the reply. "We are also running low on water but we will take half the crew."

The fifteen of us gathered anxiously at the main gangway and cast lots for who was going and who remained. The captain, mate, and five others including me were the lucky ones to go. But the captain's wife was not among them. This was too for much me so I spoke up and said:

"I will remain here to let the captain's wife go." For as anxious as I was to get home to my parents (who believed I was lost in the Lady Grant) I could not bear to see the captain and his wife separated after all they had endured together. The captain's wife was very grateful to me, and once the lucky seven got aboard the Esther, she begged the other captain to take me as well. He showed her kindness and the boat was sent back for me.

"I've left some papers," shouted our skipper across the water, "send them to me with the boy."

I looked around the town.

I was getting into the bows when the mate came out with the papers. He flung them into the boat without saying anything. As we pulled away from the schooner, the skipper of the Fanny looked over the side of the vessel and called out:

"I'm very glad to be rid of you because you have brought nothing but bad luck while aboad."

And truly it did seem like bad luck was following us, for the next morning there was trouble between six of my shipmates since food and water were scarce. The captain of the brig was annoyed.

"If you don't stop rushing around the boat, I'll clap the lot

Shipwrecks and Bush Felling

of you in irons," he threatened.

"Water, we need water," said the mate.

"I'll give you a small allowance of water each," said the captain.

As soon as they received their ration of water everything settled down, and there was no further need to put anyone in irons. I was not part of the trouble for the captain's wife had brought me a bottle of water.

"Be careful with it," she said, "we may run short. And cheer up m'lad for the captain says, 'if the wind lasts, we will be in Falmouth in forty-eight hours,' so you will soon see your parents."

Four days later we sited Land's End of old England and got into Falmouth safely. After bidding the crew of the brig farewell, our captain said:

"Tidy yourself up as best you can and I will take you to the [5]Marine Society. They will send us home."

We got there, had a good feed, and a shakedown. The next day there was a steamboat going to Southampton and away we went, glad to get nearer home at any price. When we got to Southampton the captain's wife paid my fare to London and after a long journey, I reached my old home.

---

5   A British charity established in 1756.

G.R. Meredith / W.E. Hamilton

Homecoming

My mother and little brothers were wearing black and in deep mourning when I walked in the door of my dear old home.

"Hello, Mum," I said.

She let out a shriek and Thomas and Charles hid behind her skirts, for they thought they saw a ghost.

"It's alright mother, it's really me."

But I could see she did not believe me. Her face had gone white and she trembled. My father hearing the commotion ran in, and when he saw me, he also cried out, for he too thought he saw a ghost. I had some difficulty convincing them I was still living, but when they realized it was true they were overcome with joy.

"How is it you are alive?" said Dad, "The Lady Grant went down, and all hands were lost."

"That is true," I said and but for the grace of God I would have been one of them. "Fortunately, I missed my passage on her and at the last moment shipped on the Lady West instead.

Shipwrecks and Bush Felling

There was no time to write before I left."

Then my parents sent word to my older brother and sister that I was alive. We had a family reunion the next day, and after a good home-cooked meal, I gave them all the particulars of my shipwreck. As I recounted my experiences, Thomas and Charles listened to me open-mouthed, but my mother and dear old Dad wiped away tears when they thought I was not looking. Now the ordeal was over, I felt quite the hero of my story as I recounted my adventures. But when I got to the part about my faithful Carlo, and how I had to come home penniless, I broke down and wept for I was still feeling knocked up.

"Never mind that, George," said Dad, patting me on the shoulder, "let us thank God your life was spared and you are home."

His kind words gave me strength and I pulled myself together. After a week's rest and good food, I soon began to feel my old self.

"I think I will go and have a look around the town with my mates," I said, one morning to my mother.

"You can't go out looking like that," she said, looking at my shirt and trousers meaningfully.

She was right, my recent ordeal had reduced my rigout to tattered rags.

"I have a little money set by," she said, taking some coins out of a tin on the mantelpiece. "Take this and get yourself some new clothes.

I did not want to take it for I knew money was not abundant, but she insisted so I took it at last. After getting a new rigout, I began to go about the sailor's haunts to meet some of my old shipmates. They all wanted to know when I was going to go back to sea.

"I don't know," I said, "that last voyage was a nightmare."

Although my desire for the sea was somewhat dampened, I was used to vigorous activity and quickly tired of being idle. One day, to my father's delight, I said:

"Do you want a hand with the blinds today, Dad?"

My father beamed. "That would be wonderful, George."

So, at long last, I knuckled down to the life my father wanted for me. For his sake I wished to settle down, but try as I might, I could not. The thirst for adventure arose in me once again and I was eager to get back to the sea.

When I broke the news to Dad, he was not happy.

"Stay here and learn the blind making trade, George, and when you get older, you can take the business over."

"No," I said, shaking my head. "My mind is made up. I have seen something of the world and Shoreditch is too small for me now. I cannot settle ashore; I love the sea life."

Again, my father pressed me to stay, but I said:

"I am penniless and an extra expense to you at the moment. But now that I am an Able Seaman, I have the means to earn money. I hope the next time I come home that I will have a big paycheck to repay you for all the expense you have incurred because of the shipwreck."

When my father realized it was impossible to persuade to stay, he backed down and let me go. The next day I went to the shipping office.

"I am an Able Seaman and I'm looking for a ship," I told the shipping officer.

"There is a brig bound for Algoa Bay in need of a crew," he replied.

Shipwrecks and Bush Felling

"That will do me."

He handed me the necessary documents, and I put my name down to ship in the Prince as an [6]AB.

"Be ready to sail in a week's time," said the officer.

He gave me a month's pay in advance. I was very pleased for that gave me plenty of time to get my outfit, and enabled me to pay for it without further help from my dear old Dad. With a light heart I bought a good chest of clothes and got ready for another voyage.

---

[6] Able Seaman.

G.R. Meredith / W.E. Hamilton

Onboard the Prince

The Prince was a large ship and she sat well out of the water as she had a light cargo. The captain's name was Thomas and he had a good and jolly crew, which makes for a much more pleasant journey. Nevertheless, the trip was a long one and we were all glad when we reached our destination. The wind was gently blowing out of the bay when the pilot came on board to guide us in.

"How was your trip?" he asked.

"Rough with changeable weather," replied Captain Thomas, "I'll be glad to get anchored.

The words were scarcely out of his mouth when suddenly the wind grew in such strength it whipped the water into whirlpools.

"We'll have to wait," said the pilot, looking at the water twisting about. "If the vessel gets caught in a whirlpool nothing will save her. She'll have to lay-to outside the bay until we get the wind to suit."

"If we have to wait, we have to wait," said the captain,

Shipwrecks and Bush Felling

"there is nothing else we can do."

It was four days before the wind dropped enough for us to enter the bay safely. And even then, it was difficult to make headway. But by working hard all day we got to our anchorage by nightfall.

"I'm deadbeat," I said to my shipmate Jack, as I climbed into my hammock.

"We all are," said Jack, "but at least we are finally here.

The next morning dawned warm and clear. The water was as still as a mirror when the cargo boats came alongside. Then the work began again in real earnest. I did not know which was harder; battling the sea or shifting cargo.

But after two days the agent sent more boats and a lot of little fellows called kaffirs[7] none of them more than five foot in height, but very strongly built. We laughed when we saw them.

"Why are they here?" we asked the mate. "They'll be no good to work the cargo. Shifting cargo is hard heavy work."

But the mate replied, "they will show you how to load boats, I have been here before and I know what they can do."

We were not long in seeing for ourselves what they could do, in fact we had to work even harder to keep up with them. The little fellows were like a swarm of bees about the deck as they took the remaining cargo out one side of the vessel and loaded bales of wool into the other side. The way they handled those bales of wool beat all I have ever seen. Wool bales were smaller in those days and bound with iron bands. To see those little chaps knocking them about, you would think they hadn't an hour to live.

One day the mate said to me:

---

7   Pygmies.

G.R. Meredith / W.E. Hamilton

"Run aloft, George, and put a new crane line on the backstays."

"Aye, aye, Sir."

I grabbed a small round marlinspike to help me with my work and hung it around my neck so my hands would be free for climbing. But while I was doing my job, the old crane line gave way.

"Watch out, George," shouted Jack, looking up.

I made a grab for the rigging, but it was too late. The air rushed past me with sickening speed as I tumbled headfirst towards the deck. Once again, God's hand was with me. For at the last moment I managed to turn a somersault which saved me from instant death. Instead, I landed on my feet and hurt them so badly I could not walk for two months. But worse still, the small end of the marlinspike caught me under the jaw and took away a piece of my jaw bone.

Jack was shaking as he ran over to me.

"You are a lucky lad," he said, taking the marlin spike away, "if that spike had gone the other way it would have gone right through your lungs."

He tried to help me up, but I cried out in pain when my feet touched the deck. So, he carried me to the captain. When Captain Thomas saw my injuries, he took me ashore to see a doctor, and the doctor sent me to an old kaffir woman. The old woman bandaged my wounds and nursed me for two weeks. At the end of the time I was glad to be back onboard the Old Prince once more. I crawled about the decks with my bound feet lifted up, so as not to touch the planks; for they were so painful I could not bear them to touch anything.

"I've made something for you to sit on so your feet won't

Shipwrecks and Bush Felling

have to touch the deck," said the carpenter, putting a tall stool beside me.

"And until your feet are mended, you're on light duties," said the mate kindly.

From then on, I spliced ropes and mended sails. I got on alright and was never idle. Moreover, the hands were very good to me, from captain to cabin boy, but I was grieved to find myself helpless for so long.

Throughout my ordeal, the crew and the Kaffirs continued energetically loading the cargo. When most of the wool was aboard, there came a bluster that stopped work.

It was funny to see those little pygmies clearing off to the shore. They leapt into the lighters like a lot of monkeys.

"Look at those little chaps jumping into the lighters," I said to Jack, laughing.

"They look like a lot of monkeys" chuckled Jack.

That night, (20/09/1854) the sea began to roll in the bay and the big ropes strained against our two anchors.

"I don't like this," said the captain, looking uneasy.

"We'll be alright, Captain," the mate assured him, "the rope is strong."

He was quite right and the old ship braved it fine although every man had to do his best to keep her safe. While we were all working hard to keep the vessel off the rocks, troopship the Charlotte bound for India came in for freshwater.

"I fear for that ship," said the captain, as she battled her way into the bay. "She would be better to lay-to."

And so she would have been, for she got caught in a devilish whirlpool and left her bow in those fearful rocks.

"Isn't there anything we can do?" I asked the mate.

G.R. Meredith / W.E. Hamilton

"No, George, there is not," said the mate, shaking his head sorrowfully. "If we put a boat out, it will immediately be driven onto the rocks."

It was terrible to have to stand there helplessly watching. One-hundred and seventeen souls (including eleven women and twenty-six children) were swept away that night and lost.

To our relief the old Prince weathered the storm wonderfully, and as soon as the weather improved the pygmies came aboard again. Each lighter only carried a half load this time, however, as the sea was still very rough and the agent would not send a full load until the sea was calm. I could not help laughing as I watched the little pygmies hopping around those bales.

"Are your feet feeling better, George?" asked Jack, hearing me laugh.

"No," I said, pulling a face, "but the pygmies are so funny they take my mind off my feet. They look like they are playing football with the wool-bales."

It took two months of hard work (even with the little kaffirs helping) before we were loaded and ready for the sea again. The weather was very warm, so when the boats containing stores came alongside there was only a little fresh meat. Instead, there were casks of good salted pork. When the stores were in, the pilot came aboard. He guided us skillfully out of the treacherous bay and only left when all danger was past. Once we were out at sea, the command came to put up all the sails. Then we were flying before the wind with every stitch of canvas bulging out.

We saw several outward bounders[8] on the way home and had grand weather. Everything went very smoothly until we came

---

8   Ships coming out of ports.

Shipwrecks and Bush Felling

near the Channel where we came close to the outward bounders and had to keep a good lookout both day and night until we got to the Downs of old England. We landed at Gravesend early the next morning, let down our anchors and went to bunk for we were exhausted. When we awoke refreshed, all we could think of was home and what we were going to do with our big checks. We took the next tide for London, got out as far as Deptford and anchored there waiting for another tide to take us into the docks. As soon as we came to the wharf, the dock man took charge, and our voyage was finished. Once we got our pay, we dressed in our best, shouldered our sea chests, and went ashore; some to wives, some to mothers, and some to boarding houses. That finished the voyage of the Prince, a journey that was supposed to have lasted nine months but took twelve months to the day.

G.R. Meredith / W.E. Hamilton

Runaways

My family were overjoyed to see me once again.

"You look well," said my mother kissing me.

My dear old Dad was pleased to see me, and my younger brothers hung on my every word as I recounted my adventures.

"Tell us about the pygmies again," begged Thomas and Charles.

"I have already told you about them three times," I laughed.

"Tell us again," said Charley.

So, I told the stories again. I even hopped around demonstrating how the little chaps kicked the wool bales about, as my feet were completely healed.

"What happened to your jaw, George?" said my mother.

I would have preferred not to have told them of the mishap with the crane line. But the mark on my jaw (which I bare to this day) made it impossible.

After I told them of the accident, the room became very somber and quiet as my family contemplated my narrow

Shipwrecks and Bush Felling

escape from death.

"Let me tell you about the pygmies, again," I said to lighten the mood.

As nice as it was to see my family, by now I was seventeen with six years of seafaring experience. Despite the danger and hardships, I felt bonded to sea life, and it was not long before I was keen to be off once more.

I went to the docks and met up with my mate Jack.

"Look there is a ship in Liverpool wanting a crew," said Jack, pointing to a notice on a billboard.

The idea seemed good to me, so we answered the advertisement.

The Star was a large full-rigged ship and she wouldn't be setting sail for a month which suited us. We signed up and went home again before reporting to Liverpool.

The first hint that there was a problem was the sailor who said:

"I say, you're not going on that ship, are you?"

"Yes, what of it? Is the ship unsound?"

"No, the ships alright. It's the captain and the mate, they're no good."

"No good?"

"Proper bullies they are. If you can get out of working on that ship, you would do well too."

We heeded the warning and went to the shipping office to pull out.

"I'm sorry," said the officer, looking at our papers. "These have been signed in London so there is nothing you can do. You are bound by the contract to serve on the Star."

"I suppose that is why they were advertising in London not

Liverpool for a crew," I said to Jack.

"Well, there is nothing for it," he said, shaking his head, "we must go through with this and hope for the best."

Once aboard, it was not long before we discovered for ourselves that the accusation of bullying was all too true. We were put on short rations and made to work as slaves.

"I'm dead beat from all the extra hours," Jack said one night, as we hung side by side in our hammocks, "but I'm so hungry I can't get to sleep."

"Me too," I said. "If I could get the key to the storeroom, I would break in there. I have never been of a ship that is so stingy with food. I feel faint with hunger all day."

"I think I could pick the lock," said Jack, "I used to do that sort of thing when I was a kid."

I looked around our sleeping shipmates with rising hope.

"Nobody else is awake, we could go now," I said.

"It's worth a shot," said Jack. "If we are caught, though, I hate to think what the captain will do to us."

"I for one, am willing to take the risk I'm so hungry," I said.

"Come on then," said Jack.

We crept to the storeroom and luck was on our side. Nobody stirred and Jack got the door open without too much bother. We both felt much better once we had our stomachs full. After that we went every night, and by some miracle were not caught. But one night when we were close to port our luck finally ran out and the captain caught us.

"As soon as we tie up at the dock, you will both be going to jail for theft," he snarled, laying a heavy hand on us, "and you can stay there until you rot."

I have no doubts he would have carried out his threat if we

Shipwrecks and Bush Felling

had given him the chance to do so. Instead, Jack and I along with some others stole a boat one dark night and snuck ashore. By dawn the other runaways had gone up country with cattle drivers who wanted more drovers. Jack and I did not go with them for we had come across the Second Mate of the Lance; a barque lying in the harbour. It was an American vessel greatly in need of crew. The second mate knew we were on the run but he said:

"The Lance is looking for crew. If you hide until nightfall, I'll get you on board."

He gave us a little food tied in a cloth and we cleared out of the town and hid further along the beach (about a quarter of a mile from the wharf.) We spent an anxious day afraid the police would be after us. But we learned afterwards they followed the runaways upcountry, thinking we were all together. Once the coast was clear, our new friend smuggled us onto the barque.

"Follow me," he said, when we were safely aboard, "I'll take you to meet Captain Clarke.

"Who are these men?" asked the captain, as we stood before him.

"The first mate told me to scout around and find as many hands as I could," said the second mate. "So, I brought back these sailors who have taken French leave of the Star."

"Why are you running away?" said the captain, "running away is a serious offence."

"I have been on many journeys and have never been treated so badly," I said. "Both the captain and the mate of the Star are bullies and they treated us like slaves. They cut our rations and extended our hours."

"Large numbers of crew do not run away unless there is a

big problem," said Jack.

Captain Clarke nodded and replied:

"The quarrel between you and the captain of the Star is nothing to do with me. If the first and second mate are happy with you, I have nothing to say against it."

We thanked him and followed the second mate to the forecastle.

"All you have to do is to low lie until we get out of the harbour," he said. "Don't be afraid, remember you are on an American vessel, our skipper would not allow the police to come on board so you are quite safe."

We rigged up a place in the lumber-room and the second mate lowered our food down from the hatch at mealtimes.

"Already I like this ship more than the Star," said Jack, tucking into his dinner.

"Yes," I agreed, taking a bite of a freshly baked roll. "They are not stingy on food and the captain seems a good man."

Our first impressions proved correct. The captain was a fine man and ran a good ship. He and everyone in authority were kind, and there was always plenty of food. Once we were well away from the harbour, the second mate called us out of hiding.

"You'll be alright now," he said.

"This is a beautifully shaped vessel," I said, climbing out the hatch and looking around.

"Yes, she is a beauty," said the second mate (whose name was Tod). "She was built for speed and carrying slaves to South America."

"A slave ship!" exclaimed Jack.

"Not now," said Tod. "She was seized by the Government and sold to a shipowner of Salem, fifteen miles from Boston.

Shipwrecks and Bush Felling

"Where is she headed?" I asked.

"An island called Cayenne. It's a French convict settlement. We have a five-year contract from the French Government to carry cattle to the island."

"How long does it take to get there?" said Jack.

"About six weeks. We have only got nine months left before the contract runs out, so that is about seven or eight trips. The pay is not bad, thirty dollars a month, but you'll find shipping cattle is not an easy job."

And he was right. Each run started with seventy of the crew going upcountry to bring down the cattle, big wild beasts with long horns. The men drove them into a stockyard built at the low tide mark near the wharf. When the tide was coming in, black men went in amongst them. Each man seized a beast by its horns and pulled it towards a waiting boat. Then he held its head at the side of the boat while another man paddled the canoe. The animal swam alongside until they came to the vessel.

"Throw down a rope," they called, when they got close enough.

Then the crew threw down a rope sling which was put around its horns. Up the beast came and down it went into the hold before it had time to kick. While this was going on, another mob of cattle were being put into the yard ready for the next high tide. It was all done so quickly that we got a hundred animals in the hold at a time. In this way we managed to get two hundred loaded on two incoming tides. Then we set sail. All fared well with the cattle until we were becalmed.

"I don't like this," said the captain, "speed is essential in this business. If we don't get moving soon, we will lose cattle."

G.R. Meredith / W.E. Hamilton

But day after day the wind did not come and we sat on the water going nowhere. Thirty out of the two hundred cattle died before we got to our destination. We threw the dead ones overboard and it was awful watching the sharks tearing them to pieces.

"Captain Clarke must be taking this hard," I said to Tod, "as a part-owner he must stand the loss of the cargo."

"No," said Tod, "lucky for him the Government stands the losses, not the owners of the vessel."

"When we got to Cayenne, we hauled the cattle out of the hold and floated them to the beach in the same way we got them.

On our last voyage, however, things were a little different. Once the cattle were unloaded, we had to get the ship ready for her new cargo.

"The stalls are the property of the French Government," said the first mate. "So, your first job, men, is to knock the cattle stalls apart and load the timber on the raft."

"Aye, aye, Sir," we said.

We had a tough time knocking these stalls to pieces and slinging them over the side of the ship onto a waiting raft. Black men floating in canoes, caught the slings, stacked the lumber on the raft, and towed it to the shore.

"I'm glad to see the last of all that government rubbish," I said, as we slung the final load over the side of the Lance. "The last ten days have been tough."

"I'm looking forward to getting back to our normal work," said Jack.

"Well, you will have plenty of that for the next few days," said the first mate. "We have a lot to do to make the Lance

Shipwrecks and Bush Felling

shipshape and seaworthy before taking in our next cargo."

We worked in haste to get the ship's gear in order. All the time we spliced ropes and mended sails, we kept one eye on the sky, because without cargo we were light in the water, which was dangerous should the weather turn bad. But fortune favoured us. The weather stayed fine and in due time we were ready to receive our new cargo. Then large lighters filled with boxes of merchandise came alongside the ship and we started loading up. Every box we put in the hold, and every inch we sank lower in the water, made us feel safer. When the last box went in, we battened down the hatches, hauled up the anchor and set off. It must have been a fine sight for people on the shore to see the old Lance sailing out of the harbour in full sail, for she was a pretty vessel seen under these conditions.

G.R. Meredith / W.E. Hamilton

America

We had a fair wind and it was smooth sailing until we got to the American coast. From then on in, we battled headwinds and heavy seas until we sighted the New Orleans coast. We did not stay in sight of land for long, however, for a hard wind came on again and we had to put out to sea for safety. After some shaking up, we got a fine wind along the American coast.

"We will not take long to get to Boston with this wind behind us," said the first mate pleased.

The wind stayed favourable, and as predicted, we landed in Boston a few days later.

The dock man took charge of the vessel until she was unloaded. Meanwhile, the captain paid the crew for their services and they went home, for they were from Boston.

"What about you two?" he asked Jack and I. "Do you want to be paid out now or would you help run the Lance to Salem?"

"I like her too well to leave before I'm obliged to," I said.

"I will also stay on," agreed Jack.

The captain was pleased with our answer, as it was hard to

Shipwrecks and Bush Felling

get men for short runs.

"Take a look around Boston and be back in two days," he said.

We thanked him and did as he instructed. When we returned to the ship, we found it a hive of activity. It took ten days to unload and a further ten days to reload. It seemed strange to see others unloading the ship. We did not sit about idly watching them work, however.

"Have you ever painted a ship before?" asked the captain.

"No," said Jack and I, shaking our heads.

"Well, now's your chance." He showed us how to dip the tip of the paintbrush in the paint and how to apply it in long swipes.

I was pleased to get the opportunity of learning another skill and found this knowledge useful later in life. After twenty days of this, the ship looked smart and the cargo was loaded. But in order to get to Salem we had to go fifty miles out to sea to clear the headland, and the captain found he could not get a full crew.

"It's a long way with so few men," he said, looking worried.

But we all spoke up and volunteered to do our best with the crew we had.

"Alright then," he said, smiling. He turned to the cook. "Cook, assist all you can but don't neglect the cooking."

I was not surprised by his comment, for the Americans were fond of good food and we had the best of everything, hot rolls and coffee for breakfast, and roasted and boiled meats with puddings for other meals. As far as food went, there was nothing to complain about.

So, with a skeleton crew we set off. We cleared the headland alright and were sailing nicely out to sea when we struck bad weather, and were driven into a bay about twenty miles to the south.

"Is this, Quincy bay or Hingham Bay?" shouted Jack, over the wind and waves.

"I don't know," the second mate shouted, I've lost my bearings. "I think we've been blown about twenty miles south so it might be Cape Cod."

This was serious for many ships have been wrecked there. Fortunately, we were not one of them, for we managed to ride the storm out and arrived at our destination without mishap. As we neared Salem, the pilot came aboard to guide us into the harbour. He maneuvered the ship as close as he could to the dock and when the tide was on the turn, he pulled her to the wharf and made her fast to a large post. Then he put the other end to the windless and we heaved away, cheerily singing:

"Come, all you young fellows who follow the sea,"
"To me WAY, aye, BLOW the man down,"
"Now pray pay attention and listen to me,"
"GIVE me some time to BLOW the man down!"

When we had finished, we cleared up the decks, tidied our clothes, and went ashore.

This ends my experience of the Lance, the best captain, officers, and boat of my sailing life. When we got ashore at Salem, the captain took us to the owners to get our pay.

"Well lads," said the owner, "your captain has been telling me of all your troubles and has given you such a good character, I am going to pay you thirty dollars a month for the time you

Shipwrecks and Bush Felling

were in the cattle trade. But I will leave the captain to settle the rest with you." He smiled. "I think you will be well pleased with what he gives you."

"Now George," said Captain Clarke, "you and your mates have done more than your duty, so I am giving you fifty dollars for the passage to Boston and thirty dollars for the run to Salem." He handed us two-hundred-and-seventy dollars which we proudly put in our little canvas bags."

Then we thanked him heartily and said we hoped to have as good a captain on our next voyage.

G.R. Meredith / W.E. Hamilton

Goodbye England

I went to the bank and got all but twenty dollars of my wages turned into English money, for I intended to go home as soon as I could, but I did not know when I would get another ship. Two of my mates kept all their dollars in American money as they were going to see their married sisters who lived in the States.

"Come with us, George," they urged.

"Thanks, mates, but no," I said. "I am anxious to get home again to see my dear old parents."

The next day we parted. Tears rushed to my eyes as I bid them goodbye, for we were more like three brothers than friends and I knew we would never meet again.

After they were gone, I felt very lonely. But as I strolled down the wharf, I came across a large vessel.

"Ahoy there, my name is George Meredith, is the captain looking for crew?" I called up to a sailor.

"Come on board," he called back, "I'm Jim and I will take you to the captain.

Shipwrecks and Bush Felling

The captain was very hospitable. He gave me a good dinner and told me the vessel was the Ganymede of New Brunswick, Canada.

"She is loaded with timber and bound for London," he said. "I need to get the cargo away as soon as possible but if I don't get enough men, I won't be allowed to sail, so get your stuff and come back quickly. And if you have any mates looking for a ship, bring them along with you."

After dinner I went onshore, banked my money in an international bank, and collected my sea chest. But when I came up the gangplank, the first mate stopped me.

"Hey, where are you going?" he demanded.

"I am shipping to London as one of the crew," I said.

"Let me see your ticket?"

I gave him my ticket with confidence, for Captain Clarke had given me a good recommendation.

He read it before handing it back to me.

"Alright, you'll do," he said, waving me on.

I was put to work immediately. While we were busy getting things in order, a covered wagon arrived carrying ten sailors who were so drunk they were unable to walk the decks.

"Get them on board," said the captain.

"Aye, aye, Sir."

Dragging those men out of the wagon reminded me of the black men going into the stockyards to grab cattle. Jim and I half carried and half dragged a man up the gangplank.

"He's been on the spree as usual," said Jim, as we dumped him on the deck.

"Is this normal?" I asked, looking at the ten men sleeping where they had fallen.

"Oh yes. This is the only way the captain can get these ones back for duty. They won't come until they are forced to, and the captain can not get clearance to go without his full crew."

I found this most irregular. Nevertheless, because of the captain's drastic actions we got away in due time. After the pilot had taken us out to sea, we had a good wind and the Ganymede did some swift travelling. Five weeks later we were in London.

"Goodbye," I said to the officers as I left the ship. "Thank you for your kindness. I am sorry I wasn't more helpful on the voyage."

"It's not your fault, George," they said, "anyone can get dysentery."

Once more I saw my loved parents. I took Jim with me as he knew no one in London. My mother gave him a warm welcome, treating him just like me since he was an orphan and had never known the love of a mother.

"Any friend of my son is a friend of mine," she said, "you can stay here as long as you like."

"But I am penniless and can't pay you," said Jim.

"That doesn't matter in the least, lad," said my Dad. "Consider this your home whenever you are in London."

"How's business?" I asked my father.

"Ah, none too good, George, I'm sorry to say."

"This will help you out," I said, handing him my earnings from the Lance.

"Thank you very much, son," said my father, with tears in his eyes. "I'm very grateful."

"Now tell us your latest adventures," said Charles.

"Why, do you want to go to sea?" I asked, clapping him on

Shipwrecks and Bush Felling

the shoulder.

"Maybe," said Charles. "I'm ten now, only one year younger than you, when you went off."

"May the Lord have mercy on me," said my mother, throwing up her hands in horror. "It's bad enough having one son in constant peril."

I took over the steering.

"Tell us some stories," said Charles, ignoring my mother's outburst.

"Yes, do," said Thomas.

So, I told them about the terrible time I had on the Star.

G.R. Meredith / W.E. Hamilton

"The captain and the first mate were bullies. They kept us on short rations and worked us like slaves. In the end it was so bad many of us ran away."

By the time I had finished the account of those difficult days, Charles was not so keen on the idea of going to sea. Then Jim told stories of his journeys and everything went along so merrily, Thomas and he became fast friends.

But after a good holiday, Jim and I hankered for the sea again. One morning we went down to the docks to see what the shipping was like. We found seven fine vessels lined up alongside one another. At the shipping office, an advertisement caught our eye.

"Hey look at this, George," said Jim.

"Wanted for the ship Aerolite of Glasgow," I read aloud. "Eighteen able seamen, a cook and steward, bound for Melbourne to sign articles on the 20th of November 1855."

"Melbourne! What about it, George?" said Jim. "Wouldn't it be good to see Australia."

As Jim was bent on going, I decided to sign up with him. We both went to the office and shipped in the Aerolite for four dollars per month with a month's pay in advance. Then we packed our clothes in our sea chests. We said goodbye to my family and by the end of the month were sailing down the Thames with a tug on either side of us. Little did I realize as we slid along the familiar route, that it was my final trip along the Thames. Another heavy tug joined us when we reached Gravesend beach, and the mud pilot left as the sea pilot came aboard to guide us to Lands' End. After he left, I took over the steering. For a moment I looked back and saw the last of old England. Then I turned my face to the sea and headed South.

Shipwrecks and Bush Felling

Sailor's Hell

We had a strong wind after the pilot left us, which before long blew into a gale.

"I don't like this, George," said the captain, "we are close to the coast. Get as far out to sea as you can, we don't want to be blown onto the rocks."

We certainly were in a dangerous position, but the Aerolite was a good boat. No matter how heavy the sea, she shipped very little water and sailed over the ocean like a duck. In fact, she was the best boat I was ever in for riding over heavy seas. And a good thing it was for us, as you will see later. Once we got well away from the coast, the risk of being dashed against the rocks disappeared, but the sea became so rough and uncertain that the captain said:

"Keep heading windward and try to run into a port, George."

I tried, but it was impossible for she drifted leeward into the current, which drew her into the Bay of Biscay where the sea was just awful. To make matters worse, that dreaded Bay was only forty fathoms deep and the waves rose like mountains at the head of the bay where the north and south sea meet. It takes a good ship to hold her own in conditions like this. Old sailors say that thirty ships out of every hundred are lost in this way.

"The sailor's hell, that's what we call this," said old Albert grimly. "The London was lost in this bay because of seas like this."

I was sad to hear of the fate of the old London, for she was the first ship I ever sailed in, and I did not like the thought of this one going down. For five days we battled horrific seas, but our good old ship faced them bravely. After a further fifteen days of awful seas, it calmed down a bit. The wind, however, still hung on and the sea remained bad. Throughout the whole time, two men were posted at the wheel, for it took two of us to hold it. I was at the wheel with a shipmate when the first mate called:

"Now grip her, George, hold fast with all of your strength."

I shall never forget the grip of the wheel that meant so much to our safety. I held on with my strength drawn to the utmost, aware that if we hit a wave broadside, the sea would sink us. Despite the danger, it was something grand to see this noble vessel fighting the sea, while she strained her upper gear against the elements. The first mate was so pleased with my work he kept me at the wheel for the whole time we were in the bay. Even when the wind dropped to a steady breeze and the open sea calmed down, it was still blowing hard in the bay. The only thing we could do was to run her before the seas as fast as it would allow us. We dare not put her about in the usual way.

"It's a great risk," said the first mate, "but it is the only chance we have."

Shipwrecks and Bush Felling

He was proved right, for the Aerolite toppled over the seas majestically while we did our best to save her. After battling for about twenty days, we began to give up hope of ever getting out of the bay alive. Then, to add to our difficulties, there came another bluster, dead in our teeth. The seas rolled in with a vengeance, and it looked as if they meant to settle the old ship once and for all.

"Get the lifeboats ready," commanded the captain.

So, we stocked the boats with a good supply of water, food, blankets, and oilskin coats. In the captain's boat, we added a tin-box containing the ship's papers and charts and other gear in case they might be needed.

Thank God we did not need them for that purpose, for I don't think we could have survived the heavy seas, but it seemed our only hope.

My pen trembles in my hand when I remember how feeble our hopes were as we stuck to the vessel and steered her over those mountainous seas. Seared into my memory is the awful plunge which carried away her foretopmast.

"Watch out!" came the shout, as her gear fell down around us.

"All hands on deck," shouted the mate, "clear the decks."

Then the captain and the first mate and everyone else began cutting away the gear and throwing it overboard.

The seas were so violent, two men were barely enough to hold the wheel. I was still gripping on with all my strength and the second mate was there to help me.

By now we also had a tackle on each side of the wheel, which was a great help to us. When we got to the bottom of the plunge, I thought we might never come up again, but to my relief our gallant ship rode up the other side.

"The strain on the gear is dreadful," shouted the captain, "watch out for the other mast, it could go any time."

As dreadful as that would have been, it was the rollers we feared most, for if they hit us broadside, we would founder at once.

The second mate and I lashed ourselves to the wheelhouse and held on as roller after roller bore down on us. The old boat fought hard. A wave lifted so suddenly, I thought her bows would never rise again, but she grandly lifted her nose and rose with it. The lift was so great the main topmast snapped. Yet still the good old ship was not beaten. She rocked over the wave and away she went.

I think that was the largest sea we had. By the end of our pummeling, nothing apart from the three lower masts were left standing; and they were iron, made after the style of large pipes that are used for carrying water.

After twenty-six days in this dilemma, the wind lessened and the weather cleared up. Naturally, we were keen to get out of this treacherous bay as fast as possible.

We set sail with what we had left, cleared up the decks, and made for sea again with hopeful hearts.

On the thirtieth day at about three o'clock, the man at the lookout cried:

"A lighthouse!"

"All hands on deck," shouted the first mate. "Set every stitch of canvas."

We cheered and our voices rang out in song as we hauled the sails up.

Shipwrecks and Bush Felling

"Now when I wuz a little boy so my mother told me,"
"Way haul away, we'll haul away Joe!"
"That if I didn't kiss the gals me lips would grow all mouldy,"
"Way haul away, we'll haul away Joe!"

It was a grand thing to watch the wind fill the sails and see the old ship doing her best to get as far away from that bay as possible. We hoped never to see it again.

G.R. Meredith / W.E. Hamilton

Escape and New Friends

After surviving Sailor's Hell, the rest of the trip to Australia seemed uneventful. The weather turned favourable and we made good speed. We saw a few trade vessels but they couldn't keep up with us, for although the Aerolite was not good with headwinds, she was a swift ship when she had a fair wind behind her. We landed in Melbourne seventy-five days after our ordeal.

Melbourne was rampant with gold-fever when we arrived. We had two days' leave and everywhere the talk was all about gold and gold-digging. By the time we got back to the ship we were gold-mad and desperate to get away. A group of us gathered in the forecastle, our minds fixated on gold.

"I don't want to carry on to China," said Jim, "I want to get off here and make my fortune."

"Me too," I said.

There was a general murmur of agreement.

Shipwrecks and Bush Felling

"I went to see some of the diggings and got a couple of good-sized nuggets," said a man named Charlie Clark, "I'm going to take French leave and try for more."

"Are you crazy," said Jim, "the Police are on the lookout for runaway sailors."

"I can get you away, if you really want to go," said Clark, tapping his nose furtively.

"How?"

We leaned forward and listened attentively as he whispered:

"Go about your work for the rest of the day. Load the crates of tea and make it look like you have every intention of going to China."

We nodded.

"It's my anchor tonight. Go to your beds as usual and I will hang a rope yarn down from the hatch. Make it fast to your body, George, so when I tug, it will quickly awaken you. At seventeen hours a boat will circle the vessel. This is the police leaving after they have examined the ship. You will hear them call 'all's well,' as they go."

We nodded again.

"When you feel my tug, George, alert the others and when everyone is wide awake and ready to go, get rid of the yarn. Then come up, barefoot and follow me to the lifeboat. Divide into two groups, take a side each and carry her forward as quickly as you can, and lower her over the cat head. Haul her under the bows where you will find six oars hanging off the dolphin[9]. Take them and head towards the red light in the port quarter."

"What do we do when we get to it?" I asked.

---

9 Dolphin striker is a small spar hanging off the bow.

G.R. Meredith / W.E. Hamilton

"I'll tell you when we get there," said Clark.

We disbanded and went about our jobs in the usual manner. But when night came, there was no sleep for any of us. The police came at seventeen hours and we listened anxiously for the 'all's well' cry. Not long after that, Charlie called out:

"Eight bells below, relieve the watch," without forgetting to make the old bell sound (as a blind to the Police)

The plan went without a hitch. As soon as I felt the yarn tighten around my body, I alerted the others and within half an hour from the time the bell struck, six strong men were in a boat pulling towards the red light. We moved swiftly and silently and soon came to a fine sandy beach where we ran the boat up and made her fast to a post.

"Pair up and get away in twos," said Clark. "Make for up-country and keep apart as much as you can. There is less chance of getting caught that way."

We thanked him for his trouble and care and said goodbye. Then we scattered into the darkness. As I trudged along the edge of the road, I wished I had thought to tie my shoes around my neck for it was hard going in bare feet. Nevertheless, Jim and I walked the whole night until we came to an old shed where we settled down for a much-needed sleep. When we awoke the sun was well up.

"Let's not hang around here," I said to Jim, "the police are sure to be looking for us. I want to get as far away from Melbourne as I can."

"Yes," said Jim, "let's go as far as this road will take us."

"What's the chance of getting a feed at the first village we come to?" I said. "I'm getting hungry."

We counted up our money and found that Jim had two

Shipwrecks and Bush Felling

pounds and I had three pounds ten shillings.

"We needn't go hungry, that will last awhile," I said pleased.

The hot sun beat down on us as we tramped along the road. We saw no village, but we noticed a clear space ahead.

"I think there is water over there," I said.

"I hope so," said Jim, "I feel very thirsty and want a drink more than something to eat."

We hurried on, and sure enough we came upon a delightful [10]stream. We drank to our fill and felt much refreshed despite the lack of food. While we were resting after our drink and cooling our feet, we noticed a large bush in the distance.

"That looks like a good place to camp," said Jim, pointing at it.

"Yes, it's an ideal spot. Come on, let's go," I said, pulling my feet out of the water.

We reached our goal after sundown, and feeling tired, we lay down under a large blue gum tree and were soon fast asleep. But my feet were so painful through walking barefoot on the scorching ground, I kept waking up with the pain. During one of my wakeful patches I heard someone say:

"We won't pitch the tent for it will soon be daylight."

Then two men lay down under a tree not far from us. In the morning, they introduced themselves.

"I'm Bill and this is my mate Jeff," said Bill, running his eye over our sailor's rigouts. "I suppose you blokes are on French leave and after gold."

Jim and I shot a glance at each other.

"It's alright, you don't have to worry about us," said Jeff, clapping me on the shoulder. "Bill's a sailor too."

---

10   Probably Bendigo Creek.

G.R. Meredith / W.E. Hamilton

We gathered up some dry sticks lying nearby and made a small fire. Jeff put a [11]billy of water on top, and while we waited for it to boil, we talked of ships and swapped tales of sea life. Naturally, the talk wound around to the subject of gold. It turned out they were diggers who had found gold in the creek we had taken our drink from.

"This morning we're going back to stake out our claim," said Bill, stirring tea into the boiling pot.

"If you pay your share of the expenses, you could join up with us if you like," said Jeff, cutting a loaf of bread into four and handing us a chunk each.

"And camp alongside us," said Bill.

This suggestion pleased Jim and me, so we agreed and said: "Thank you very much."

"Now that is settled," said Bill, when we had finished breakfast, "we'd best be off, for a rush of diggers will be here soon, and we must get our claim fixed up before the mob arrives."

We nodded, threw dirt over the fire, and went back to the creek.

---

11 An enamel pot with a lid and a wire handle.

Shipwrecks and Bush Felling

Gold Fever

Once we got to the creek Bill and Jeff pegged out their claims.

When they were finished, Bill handed me his tomahawk.

"Take this and cut some pegs," he said, "and then knock them in here and here."

He pointed out the best spot for our claim. While we were banging pegs into the ground, our new friends pitched their tent. When we were finished, Jim and I chose a nice tree stump beside them as our resting spot.

"Tomorrow," said Bill, as the sun slid under the horizon, "we will show you how to find gold.

Looking for gold was not complicated and Bill was a good teacher. Seeing how simple it was, Jim and I got into the creek and set to work for ourselves. Systematically, we turned over rocks and lifted stones from the bed of the stream. Suddenly Jim called out:

G.R. Meredith / W.E. Hamilton

"Come here, George, I see something shining under this big rock!"

"It looks the same colour as a fifty-dollar piece," said Jim, calling the others over.

"There's a nibble here," said Bill, squinting into the water. "Get your matchbox ready." They heaved up the stone and we picked up small gold pieces the size of shot. When we had finished, we had three-and-a-half boxes filled to the top with gold.

"Jolly good start," said Bill, as he dug a hole inside the tent.

Jeff transferred our hoard from the matchboxes to a pepper tin. "That's three pounds per box."

He put the pepper tin into the hole and buried it. There and then we decided to join together and form a company. Then the four of us went to work with a good heart.

"Look at the stones carefully," said Jeff, giving us the benefit of his experience, "often there is more gold in the stone than under it."

By the end of the day I was jubilant, for I had managed to fill two more boxes. Jim, however, was feeling down, for he had not found anything more.

"Don't be hard on yourself, Jim," said Jeff. "I worked for weeks once without finding any colours. That's just the way it goes sometimes. You never know when you will find something big."

The experienced digger's speech gave Jim courage, and the next day we got a nugget worth fifty pounds. After that, we usually managed to get a matchbox full each day.

We had not been working our claims long when we heard a lot of creaking and croaking, and singing and roaring in the

Shipwrecks and Bush Felling

distance.

"Hey here they come," shouted Jim. All day the noise got closer, and by night there were three-hundred men on the ground. The next morning there were a hundred men in the creek before we got started. To protect our claim, Jim and I went to our lower boundary pegs and the other two went to their upper pegs. But nobody came near us, for they were all too busy further down the creek where they were getting some good gold. By the time they had been there a week, every stone in the stream was turned upside down, the largest find was got in the spot where Jim and I had our first drink. As the numbers of diggers swelled, a big canvas store popped up.

"I'm going to see if they sell boots," I said to Jim. "My feet are very sore and tender."

"Good idea," Jim nodded, "we have been too long without them."

We were going to use the money we had in our pockets to buy them, but Bill spoke up and said:

"Hold on to your money and barter with boxes of gold."

We did as he advised and bought our boots out of the treasure in our matchboxes. In addition, we bought two pairs of socks, a pound of tobacco, and two clay pipes. A little later we bought a couple of picks, a long-handled shovel, some timber for a cradle, and two pans for washing the gravel. We were now making good wages, and tents were going up at such a rapid rate there was quite a township lining the creek. After a month there was even a public house and a bank in the main street (which had begun to look quite homely.) Life took on a routine; we worked in the creek all day and slept next to the stump at night. We had been at it for twelve weeks when I made a big discovery.

"Look over there in the side of the bank," I said to Jim, "I can see something glittering."

We used our picks and dug about at the edge of the creek.

"Here it comes," I said, as we levered my find out.

It was a two-ounce gold nugget. With this, Jim and I bought a tent and pitched it near our mates. The next morning, after a greatly improved night's sleep, we continued turning stones and found our last big find; a nugget of three ounces. Then it was back to shot sized pieces.

So, there we were, four happy mates working together and bringing home gold each night. But it wasn't all laughter and song. Many stealing loafers slunk in among us. We kept the gold we found each day in canvas belts around our bodies (for that was the only safe place) and banked the rest. One day there was a big commotion.

"What's going on?" I said.

"They've caught two fellows stealing and are going to hang them by lynch law," said the bloke in the claim next to us.

I watched as an angry crowd of diggers strung the thieves up to a branch of a tree. They hung there all day and were taken down by night and buried in a used-up claim. Despite this drastic measure, the ring of thieves continued to be a danger to the diggers and a careful watch was needed. After working the creek for six months and doing very well, something happened that put an end to my gold-digging days.

Shipwrecks and Bush Felling

Health Troubles and a Doctor's Advice

Sanitary conditions are not the best in a gold-rush-town. I did not get sick, but my eyes were giving me trouble.

"What's wrong, George?" said Jim, as we walked to the bank one day. "You keep rubbing your eyes."

"Does that man in the distance look extremely tall to you, Jim?" I asked.

"No," said Jim, "he looks about average height."

"Something weird is happening to my sight," I said. "He looks to me like he is eight feet tall, but when he gets close, he will look like a small lad."

"That is weird," said Jim. "Your eyes do look a bit red and weepy. You should see a doctor."

"Is there a doctor in the camp?" I asked the owner of the bank when we handed over our gold, "I'm having problems with my eyes."

G.R. Meredith / W.E. Hamilton

"No, you'll have to go to Melbourne."

"I don't think I could see well enough to walk all the way there," I said.

"I'll tell you what. The troopers come for the gold at the end of every month and carry it to Melbourne. If I put in a good word for you, you might be allowed to go with them."

So, at the end of the month, my mates gave me my share of our gold (which I stashed in my canvas belt) and I bid them goodbye.

The troopers were very kind to me.

"If you are willing to lead the pack horses, you can ride behind us," said the head trooper.

"I can't see much," I said.

"It won't matter," said the trooper, "your horse will follow the ones in front."

He was quite right, my horse kept so close to the others I was able to ride with my eyes closed. After three days, we reached the bank in Melbourne. Once I had dismounted, I thanked the troops and went inside to get my gold weighed and exchanged for cash. That gave me ninety-two pounds fifteen shillings. I kept what I thought I might need for the doctor, and banked the rest.

The doctor examined my eyes and announced:

"You have sand blight in a bad form, young man. Take this," he said, handing me a bottle, "and wash your eyes with it four times a day. If they don't improve, I advise you to go to New Zealand. I have been told it has the healthiest climate in the world."

As it was impossible to see small flakes of gold with my eyes in such bad condition, I hung about Melbourne for two or

Shipwrecks and Bush Felling

three months, hoping for enough improvement to go back to my pals at the diggings. But although my eyes got less painful, they did not get much better. To fill in my time, I wandered about the docks and fell in with the second mate of one of the vessels I had once sailed in. Neil was now a captain, working amongst the coasters. We got talking ship.

"I know of a fine schooner in the Yarrow river, George," he said. "It used to belong to a Russian family who intended to stay in Australia but have decided to go home."

"What of it?" I said.

"She was sold at auction the other day for a mere song, a shoemaker bought her to take passengers to New Zealand."

"A shoemaker! What does a shoemaker know about running a ship?"

"Not much, but he doesn't have to, for he has hired old Captain Travers to run her. He's looking for crew. What about it, George? I could introduce you to the Captain."

"I'll think about it and get back to you."

I left him and went straight to the doctor.

"Your eyes are not much better," said the doctor, examining them closely. "I advise you to go to New Zealand for if they do not improve soon you could go blind."

When I heard these words, I made up my mind to go.

G.R. Meredith / W.E. Hamilton

Goodbye to Life at Sea

Neil and I met Captain Travers in town and he took us to the vessel, which I found was quite a new one.

"She is a fine vessel, is she not?" said the Captain.

"She certainly is. The Hackerfield of Melbourne," I said, reading the name on the side.

"She was built in Russia for the Russian prince," said Captain Travers.

"How many crew members have you got?"

"Five hands, the cook and a steward."

"And how many passengers?"

"Ah, we have a slight problem there. I have forty passengers paying ten pounds a head and need another ten to make the trip pay."

"You won't be long finding them," said Neil, "for there are many people wanting to go to New Zealand."

"That's not the problem, I've not sufficient accommodation

Shipwrecks and Bush Felling

for them all. The owner would prefer to put the vessel in storage than payout for extra bunks. But I have a notion of how to get around the problem. How about it, George, are you interested in a job?"

I told him I was.

"Come back in a few days' time," said Captain Travers, "by then I will have sorted out my little problem."

I went to the bank and withdrew all my money, which, after paying board for so long and the doctor's expenses, was greatly reduced. But as the captain had paid me a month's wages, I was able to send it all to my parents. When I reported for duty, I found the captain had struck a deal with a merchant. In addition to our passengers, we carried a cargo of casks of beef and pork, boxes of candles and other goods, and as many kit-set wooden houses as we could take.

"With the extra income I've engaged a carpenter," said the captain. "I've given my cabin to a family and all the single men can stay in the main hatch. Your first job, George, is to help the carpenter fix up bunks down there."

Finally, after a lot of work, everyone was accommodated and onboard. We set sail and I found that Captain Travers was a good hand at coasting, so we made a good passage. The air got crisper as we got closer to New Zealand and I could feel my eyes getting better and better the further away from Australia we got. While we were sailing, I let it slip to a mate I was thinking of taking French leave when we got to New Zealand.

"Go to Kaiapoi," he said. "There's a Maori trading post there, they will give you a job cutting firewood."

I filed his advice in the back of my head for a later time. Our first stop was Otago, where we landed six families and some of the houses. Then we went on to Lyttleton, which was our final port of call. By now my eyes were almost completely better and I felt invigorated. As we sailed up the Lyttleton harbour I was so taken up with the appearance of the place and the country in general, I decided to give up the sea and settle down in New Zealand. It was November 1853, exactly a year after my terrible time on the Aerolite in the Bay of Biscay. I helped unload the cargo as if I had no intention of skipping off, and when we were finished, the captain (who was feeling generous after a good time with an old friend in the public house) gave me five shillings and said:

"Have a good look around, George, and tomorrow I will call for you at the pub."

"Thank you, Sir," I said.

When no one was looking, I gathered my belongings and some food from cook (for which I gave him two and sixpence). Then I muttered goodbye to the schooner and left.

Once more I was free of ships. I left my luggage at the hotel, hoisted my [12]swag onto my back and set off up the steep bridle path.

---

12   A billy, frying pan, pipe, and tucker bag rolled into a canvas bedroll.

Shipwrecks and Bush Felling

New Zealand

I was anxious to get away from Lyttleton as the police were on the prowl for runaway sailors. I walked as quickly as I could up the steep path and by sundown, I was well over the Port hills. On the other side I found level ground but no roads, just a bullock track leading to the place where Christchurch now stands. I made for the track and followed it for about two miles until I came to a lot of manuka scrub. Feeling tired and hungry, I thought, 'here's a good place for the night.'

I pulled my ship's knife out of my pocket and cut a quantity of scrub which I laid under my bedroll. Then I made a small fire, had a good feed and slept soundly.

The sun awoke me early the next morning. I rubbed my eyes, sat up and had a good look round. 'Well my lad' I said to myself, ''tis farewell to the sea and hello to a new career on the land'.

In front of me stretched a vast plain with a thin track winding for miles through [13]toetoe, tussock and cabbage trees.

---

13   A tall grasses native to New Zealand.

G.R. Meredith / W.E. Hamilton

I rolled up my swag and set off down the track. After I had walked a considerable distance, I spotted a tent, and making for this I found a woman inside.

"Good Day Madam," I said, "Where will this track take me? I want to get to Kaiapoi?"

"You're going the right way," she said, "stick to the track and you'll get there."

I thanked her and set off again but she called out:

"Come back, lad, have a bite to eat."

She gave me a good meal and a cup of tea, which cheered me up considerably.

Lyttleton Harbour.

After bidding my new friend goodbye, I continued my journey and got to the Maori post that night. I knew nothing of the Maori tongue, but there was a boy who could speak English. Through him, the Ngai Tahu tribe welcomed me and

Shipwrecks and Bush Felling

offered me a makeshift bed.

"They want you to meet them in the bush tomorrow morning," said the boy.

I gave him two and sixpence and said:

"Go to the store and get me a billy, a pannikin and some sugar."

"I have never held a silver piece before," he said, jumping for joy as the silver piece touched his hand.

"What do the tribe do for money then?"

"They swap firewood for goods. Get whatever you need from the store and we will pay for it with wood."

So, my life in the bush as a firewood cutter started. I built a snug little hut and got on well with the Maoris.

One day I went to the store with the boy and got a good tent, some tea and sugar, a strong pair of boots and an axe (which I needed badly.) While I was getting these articles, the storekeeper inquired where I was bound for.

"Anywhere I can get a job."

"Will you do a job for me?" he asked. "I want a cellar dug under this store, and the soil cleared away to the river at the back. I will pay six shillings a day and your tucker."

"Alright, when do you want me to start?"

"Immediately," he said, handing me a shovel.

By the time the cellar was finished, I felt the police would no longer be looking for me. Hoisting my swag onto my back, I set off to Lyttleton to pick up the belongings I had left in the hotel. My mood as I swung along the road was optimistic; I had a few pounds in my pocket, and was happy with my new life in New Zealand. I had only travelled about three miles when I met a bullock dray going over the Port Hills.

G.R. Meredith / W.E. Hamilton

"Ahoy there," I called, "could I trouble you for a lift?"

"Climb on up," said the driver, "I'd be very glad of your company."

I threw my swag into the back of the dray and sat on it.

"Where have you come from?" asked the driver.

"Melbourne," I said, tapping tobacco into my pipe.

"Melbourne," exclaimed the driver, "that's where I come from." I lit my pipe, and as the dray rumbled along, we had a long yarn about Melbourne and the diggings. It was night when we reached the spot where we had to get feed for his animals. While he tended to the bullocks, I rigged up my tent. Then I lit a fire, put my billy and frying pan on it, and had dinner ready for both of us by the time he had finished. The next morning my companion said:

"Come with me, George, and see a bit of the country."

"As much as I'd like to, I can't," I said. "I have to get my belongings that I left at Lyttleton."

"It's a pity," he said.

I felt the same, but as it couldn't be helped, I rolled up my swag and with mutual thanks we parted, he one way and I the other.

When I got over the Port Hills, I halted at the hotel where I had left my luggage and booked in for a week, for I had decided to have a rest and a good look around. During that time, I fell in with a man called Lingard who asked me if I wanted work.

"I'm a contractor working on the Sumner road and I'm looking for men for road workers. If you want to join up, I'll give you nine shillings a day.

I agreed to join him after my week's stay in the hotel, and he gave me directions to his camp. The following Monday I

Shipwrecks and Bush Felling

pitched my tent in the camp and started my new task. There were twenty men. They were a decent friendly set of fellows, and we all got on well together. Among them was a man named Charlie Howard. He had been the chief steward on the ship that came to Lyttleton. I liked him greatly as he was a real nut, full of fun and mischief. Because of the comradery, the job was a pleasant one. We cut down rocks and rolled them down into the Sumner river, which ran around the foot of the Port Hills on the Christchurch side. Although I was no longer a sailor, my interest in ships remained. A small steamer making its way up the river caught my eye.

"What's the name of that vessel," I said, pausing in my work.

"That's the Almos," said Charlie. "She's come from England and takes holidaymakers up and down the river."

I waved and carried on rolling rocks. Most of the days I

worked on the road were uneventful, but on September the eleventh 1855 Sebastopol fell in the Crimean war, and it was our good fortune that Governor Brown was in port when the news arrived.

"Lingard, give the men a holiday," he said.

And as the work was government-funded, Lingard had to do as he was told. When we heard the news, all hands (including the cook) decided to celebrate the occasion in town.

"Come on, let's go to Doctor Donald's house and thank the good old Governor," shouted Charlie, picking up his fiddle and striking up a tune. So, to the melody of, 'The girl I Left Behind Me,' we all marched rank and file to where the Governor was staying. When we reached the Doctor's house, Charlie shouted:

"Three cheers for Governor Brown and the fall of Sebastopol!"

Then we let rip with cheers and shouts. The Governor came to the window waving his hat, and Doctor Donald lowered a bottle of whisky down. That started off another roar of enthusiasm and shouting. In the midst of all the fun and merriment, a boatman came running along the wharf.

"The Almos has been wrecked," he shouted, "she got caught on the bar."

We rushed down to the shore and were relieved to see the passengers stepping over the rocks to safety. No lives were lost, but the boat was a complete wreck with a large hole in her side. All told, it was an exciting end to a fun day.

I stayed working on the Sumner road until it was finished on the 24th of August 1857. Although it gave access overland to Christchurch, the general attitude towards it was fear and

Shipwrecks and Bush Felling

distrust.

"Do you think anyone will be brave enough to actually drive over it?" I said, as I packed up my tent and rolled my cooking gear into my bedroll.

"James Fitzgerald is going to drive over it," said the cook.

"The politician James Edward Fitzgerald?" I asked.

"The very same."

And he really did. We waved and cheered as the brave man made the very first trip over our road. Then I said goodbye to my mates, hoisted my swag onto my back and set off for Christchurch.

G.R. Meredith / W.E. Hamilton

Searching for Work

When I got to Christchurch, I fell in with a bushman called Ben. Ben worked in the Oxford bush near the Rakaia river about fifty miles south of Christchurch. He had an agreement with a sheep station in Alfred Forest for a big load of fencing posts.

"Come and join me," he said.

I did not much care for the man but, nevertheless, I was keen to work, so I agreed.

We trudgeed down the narrow dirt road, and by nightfall we had travelled twenty-five miles and reached the Selwyn River. We fixed our camp, had a bite to eat, and fell into a deep sleep. The next morning, we still felt tired, so we stayed put for a day and a half. At length we had recovered enough to carry on. We forded the Selwyn and got as far as the Rakaia river but did not cross it, because it was very deep and dangerous. On the other side was an accommodation house, and tied up at a small jetty was a punt.

Shipwrecks and Bush Felling

"We'll camp here," said Ben, "the punt is loaded with wood, so she'll be over here in the morning and we can catch a ride back."

"Do you think we could get a good feed over there?" I asked, unrolling my swag and looking in my tucker bag. "I've only tea and a little bread left."

"I've stayed there before," said Ben, "and they put on a good spread. In fact, it would be worth staying a couple of nights just for the food."

So that is exactly what we did. After catching a lift over the river, we stayed at the house for two days and at the end of our time I had to let my belt out a notch.

"Come on, George, we'd best be on our way," said Ben, on the third day. "If we get going now, we can make it to Alfred Forest before dark."

We tramped cross country all day until we came to Alfred Forest. But when we spoke to the station manager, he said:

"You're too late, Ben. You took so long getting back, I thought you weren't coming so I let the contract to another bloke last week."

This was a blow.

"Seeing as you have had such a long journey," he continued, "you can rest here for a few days before you move on."

"Tough luck," said Ben, as we set up camp, "but there are other jobs to be had in the bush. I think I'll stick around here and try to pick up something."

By now, however, my first impressions of the man had strengthened into dislike and I felt we would never become pals.

"I think I'll keep moving and see what comes up." I said.

We caught a lift over the river.

So, I set off alone for the next station, pleased to be rid of the man.

On my way I saw a mob of cattle coming towards me. I waited for the drover on horseback who rode in front of the herd. When he was within speaking distance I called out:

Shipwrecks and Bush Felling

"Gidday mate, I'm looking for work, do you know of anything going?"

"I'm taking the cattle to a place called Rakapuka Bush," he said, stopping his horse. "Come with me if you like. There are two stations near it, and they are building a township nearby called Geraldine. You'll likely pick up work there."

I thanked him for his offer and when his horse moved on, I wandered along with the cattle. That night we camped in a dry river bed called the Hinch and the following day we got to the Rangitata River, which we managed to cross alright.

"That's the bush over there," he said, pointing into the distance. "That's where I'm taking the cattle. It's owned by a man called Pollock."

As I gazed at the thickly wooded land, little did I think that one day I would have a sawmill in that very same bush. At length the trees loomed up around us and our ways parted.

"Good luck with the job hunt," said the drover, as he led the cattle off the road and into the heart of the bush.

"Thanks for your help," I called back.

I continued walking until I came to William McDonald's station near Geraldine.

"I'm looking for work," I said to the station manager, "are you needing anyone?"

"No, we're full up, try Mr. Nolan. He lives in a bush hut further down the road."

I carried on and when I came in sight of the hut I called out:

"Hello, is anyone home? I'm looking for Mr. Nolan."

A Maori woman came out.

"I'm Mr. Nolan's wife, he's out at the moment. He will be back later if you want to wait for him."

G.R. Meredith / W.E. Hamilton

That seemed a good idea to me. She went back into the hut and I struck up a conversation with an old chap who was putting up a cob chimney.

"Do you want a hand, mate?" I said.

"That would be grand, young fellow."

It turned out he was an old whaler called Jim Buttle. Poor Buttle came to a sad end. He was murdered a few years later on the west coast. We swapped sea stories as we worked in the afternoon sun, and the hours melted away pleasantly. Eventually a rough-looking man came down the road.

"Here comes Nolan," said Buttle, out of the side of his mouth. "Watch what you say, he's a tough one."

"Good afternoon, Sir," I said, "I'm looking for work and am wondering if you need anything done?"

"Get out of here before I set the dog on you," he roared. "I don't need nothing."

At that moment I was glad Nolan had no work for me, because he was not the sort of man I wanted to work for. I quickly moved on to the [14]Arawhanui bush and set up camp for the night. When the dawn broke, I noticed a small hut nearby. A man sat outside the hut, boiling a billy over a small fire.

"Hello there," I said. "I didn't see your hut in the dark last night. What are the chances of finding work around here?"

"Go to the Maori pa down the road and ask for Crabb," said the man, "he'll tell you what work needs doing."

I thanked him for his help, and once more rolled my swag up and hoisted it onto my shoulder. The tribe received me kindly when I arrived and put me up for the night. Crabb was a big strong Maori man who spoke English and we got on well.

---

14   About half a mile from where Temuka stands.

Shipwrecks and Bush Felling

"I've got plenty of work for several fellas," he said. "The boss is called Cranky Bill. He's away getting cattle at the moment, and he wants a stockyard built to hold them."

"What happens if he gets here before we are finished?"

"They go into Hornbooks paddock. Tomorrow we will set up camp and start cutting timber."

The next day, the two of us went into the bush. I pitched my tent and made myself comfortable as I suspected it would be a long job. Then the Maori and I got busy felling trees, and cutting out large round posts for this yard. To begin with we had the place all to ourselves because although Cranky Bill was in a great hurry to get this yard finished, he could not find more men. We were dropping a big tree one day when we heard the sound of many cattle.

"There comes Cranky Bill," said Crabb, pausing in his work.

"Is he really as cranky as his name?" I said.

"I don't know, I only see him for a few minutes when he brings us supplies."

Crabb was quite right. The whole time I was there, I only saw Bill when he brought us food and stores. He was a generous man though, he never let us want for anything. We continued working and the sound of the cattle veered away from us as Cranky Bill herded them into Hornbook's paddock. A little later he arrived with four men and a pack of food.

"I've bought you two teams of sawyers to help you out, Crabb," he said. "I would have hired more to hurry the job along but these are all the men I can get."

He dumped the pack down and bustled off. So now there were six of us. One pair of sawyers were an older man called

Jack the Russian and his younger buddy Tom Marsh. While Crabb and I continued felling trees, each team of sawyers dug a pit three-feet wide, six-feet deep and a little longer than the logs. Across this pit stout they laid sticks of timber before rolling a log onto them and chocking it in place. Then Tom climbed on top of the log, stretched a fishing line rubbed with charcoal along the outer edge, and flicked it with his fingers to leave a straight line.

"Here you go, Tom," said Jack, handing him one end of a five-foot-long two-handled saw, with enormous teeth.

Tom caught the handle and Jack disappeared into the pit. Then bending their backs in unison, they worked the saw rapidly down the line.

"Stop," shouted Jack when they came to the first cross-bearer.

Tom climbed down and Jack popped out of the pit and together they lifted the log over the bearer. Then Tom climbed back on top and Jack disappeared below again. Only Tom was visible as they undulated along the log. They carried on in this manner until they got to the end and the slice fell off. Then they turned the log over and cut another side. They repeated that two more times until the log was a long beam. Then they sawed it into strips. All the time the sawyers were working their saw in long vertical strokes, Crabb and I worked in unison, pulling our long cross-saw horizontally through the trunks of nearby trees. It was hard grueling work and I was happy when Crabb called out:

"[15]Smoko time."

We downed tools and lit our pipes as we waited for the billy

---

15   A short break.

Shipwrecks and Bush Felling

to boil. Over our tea-break, I discovered Tom was a sailor.

"I left my ship at New Plymouth in November 1852," he said, taking a bite of [16]damper. "That's exactly a year before I arrived in Lyttleton," I said.

As we talked, I found we had much in common. All too soon, smoko was over and it was back to work. It took four weeks for the six of us working from dawn to dusk to get the stockyards built. When we were finished, Bill was immensely pleased.

"That's a mighty fine job you boys have done," he said. "Come with me to Hornbook station and I'll fix you up."

So, I went with him and got what I wanted; a pair of hobnail boots, two pairs of trousers (one of Bedford cord and one of canvass) two blue jumpers, and a hat.

---

16   A bread made in the coals of a campfire.

G.R. Meredith / W.E. Hamilton

Although there was still more work available, I made up my mind to go to Dunedin and ship again, as I heard they were giving ten pounds a month to go to China. But just as I was getting ready to go, heavy rain set in for two weeks, making travelling to Dunedin impossible because of floods. As we sat in our tents with the rain drumming down, I got better acquainted with Tom Marsh and we had many talks about our sea life.

"Once the weather fines up, I'm going back to sea," I said. "I'm sick of all this changing about. I miss the comradery and routine of ship life."

"Don't do that, George," begged Tom and Jack. "Stay with us and take up pit-sawing.

At this, I felt my resolve waiver as by now the three of us had become fast friends.

"Join us, George," urged Jack. "I'm growing too old for this sort of work. I can do all the cooking and keep the blades sharp, but we need a younger man to work the pitsaw."

"Come into the pit and try your hand at cutting a white pine log," said Tom.

At their urging, I climbed down into the pit and gripped the bottom handle of the saw.

"Are you ready, George?" shouted Tom.

"Yeah."

"OK let's go."

I bent my back as I dragged the teeth of the saw through the wood. Then I straightened up as Tom lifted the saw for a second cut. He had the harder job because I had gravity on my side. What wasn't so good, however, was there was no cooling breeze in the pit. And what was worse, sawdust rained down

Shipwrecks and Bush Felling

on my head, filling my eyes, ears, and mouth. The work was gruelling but no more terrible than tree felling or sailing.

"What do you think?" I said, when we got to the end of our slice.

"Not bad for a first attempt," said Jack, looking at the plank closely.

"You'll soon get the hang of it," said Tom.

"So, what about it," said Jack, "do you want to join our team?"

"Go on, George, what do you say?" said Tom, "We'll give you one pound a week and tucker."

"As soon as this contract is over," said Jack, "I intend to give up sawing and you can have all my tools."

I looked at their friendly faces and was won over.

"It's a deal," I said, shaking their hands.

G.R. Meredith / W.E. Hamilton

Bush Felling

After Jack retired, the first contract Tom and I worked together on was an order for a large woolshed for Mrs. Rogers of Levels station. I soon became an expert at the sawing and within six months could do what I liked with the saw. I liked the work and took pride in it. Tom and I could turn out boards with hairs-breath accuracy; a very difficult thing to do. We got such a reputation for speed and accuracy nobody was willing to go against us when Tom called out:

"I challenge any bushmen to go against two sailors!"

In those days, timber was greatly in demand, in fact the demand was much greater than the supply, and we were making big money. So much so, that Tom and I banded together and bought one hundred acres at [17]Champion station for forty-five shillings per acre. We had nearly finished our contract, when two station owners, Mr. Mitchell Studholme and Mr. Haines, came up from Waimate to see us.

"Will you men come and cut timber for us?" said Mr.

---

17 Half a mile from Temuka.

Shipwrecks and Bush Felling

Haines. "We have unlimited orders for timber for we are building woolsheds and station buildings."

"Alright," we agreed, shaking hands, "we'll come when we have finished here."

"I'll send a bullock tray for you. When do you think you will be finished?" said Mr. Studholme.

We gave him an estimated time and the bullock tray arrived as we cut our last log. We packed up our tools and swags and climbed into the tray. We got to Timaru that night and camped there. In those days, Timaru was nothing more than three houses and a store surrounded by tussock and cabbage trees. Two of the houses were public houses where you could get a drink anytime, any day or night. Yanky Sam (who was an old whaler and head steersman) owned one of the pubs and Captain Cain lived in the house with his wife Jane and stepdaughter, [18]Kate.

The newly opened store belonged to Henry Le Cren and his wife, Margret. Le Cren was a fine gentleman, liked by everyone. He was honest and courteous to all who came in contact with him. He had a store and accommodation house in Lyttleton, so he sent Captain Cain to run the Timaru store. The store stocked everything from flour and soap, to rope and pickaxes. It had the smell peculiar to general stores; a mixture of lavender, oilskins, molasses, and Stockholm tar. In a small booth in one corner was the Post Office.

In the morning we went to the store to stock up on supplies. When we arrived there, Captain Cain wore a blue serge jumper and moleskin trousers tied at the knees. On his feet were heavy Crookham boots, yellow to their tops with clay, for he was

---

18   Kate's husband Thomas Hall many years later murdered Captain Cain

building a [19]cob cottage.

"Hello Gentlemen," said Captain Cain, "what can I do for you today?"

"We need six months' worth of supplies," said Jack, handing him our list.

"Whereabouts do you men hail from?" he asked, as he moved about the store collecting our requirements.

"Temuka," I said, "Tom and I have just bought a hundred acres at Champion station."

"Hold on to it," said old Yanky Sam, who had wandered into the store, "buy all you can, but sell nothing." (I wish now I had listened to his advice, for I would be a rich man by now if I had.)

"Where are you headed?" said Yanky Sam.

"To Waimate."

"You must have a big job on to need all these supplies," said Captain Cain.

"Unlimited orders," said Tom.

"Well, good luck to you," said the Captain stacking our purchases in boxes.

We paid him and continued our journey. It took a week to reach Waimate from Timaru, where we built a hut and settled down for a long stay.

"This is very heavy timber," I said, as we looked around at the huge trees towering above us. "We may have to use the sixteen-foot cross-saw!"

"I've engaged a bullock team to help you out," said Mr. Studholme.

---

19   Walls made of clay mixed with chopped tussock and horse manure.

Shipwrecks and Bush Felling

Captain Cain.

I was very pleased to hear that. Once we got started, life settled into a predictable routine. Every morning Jack got up at 4 am and cooked us a huge breakfast of porridge and meat stew. After breakfast, we felled trees and cut the trunks into logs for the bullocks until Jack blew the bullock horn to signal lunch. Lunch was jam sandwiches. Once the bullocks had dragged the logs over to the pits, away we went, sawing them into planks until dinner time. Dinner was soup, meat, and pudding. Then we worked until dark. In between meals were morning and afternoon smoko. We worked six days a week and on Sunday we did our washing and played cards. We did not have to sharpen our saws on Sunday as other bushmen did, however, because Jack kept our saws razor sharp.

The bullocks were very helpful but, unfortunately, we could only get them in the slack times of the year.

"We've only got them for a week or two," Tom said, when we heard the team in the distance, "let's stop pit-sawing and use them to make a stockpile of logs next to the pit."

G.R. Meredith / W.E. Hamilton

It seemed a smart idea to me. As it was, during the busy season we often had all our logs sawn into planks long before the bullocks were available. Then we had to roll the logs to the pit ourselves, because the alternative was to sit around idle.

"The Big Haul" by P. Parrant.

As soon as we had a stack of timber cut for the station building, the bullock drag was not long in coming. Then with Tom on top of the log, and me in the pit, away we went, sawing with all our strength to be ready with another load of planks by the time he got back. We usually kept one step ahead of the bullock driver and loaded him up as fast as he came. For twelve months we slaved away to keep the builders building. But that suited

Shipwrecks and Bush Felling

us quite well as the money was big. When Studholme was well underway with his buildings, other stations came to us with orders. Then we employed two Maori blokes to fell trees while we concentrated on pit-sawing. In this way the weeks slipped by until one day a letter came for me.

G.R. Meredith / W.E. Hamilton

My Family Arrives in New Zealand

I had not forgotten my family back in England. The letters had been going back and forth. By now my father was sixty-five and wanting to retire.

'Come to New Zealand it is a wonderful country,' I wrote often.

Finally, in 1857, I received a letter to say that he and my mother and Thomas, were sailing on the Jane Fletcher and would arrive in Lyttleton. I set off to meet them and, Tom, who had a sweetheart in Canterbury went with me. But once again the weather interfered with my resolve to meet a ship. When we got to Timaru the heavens opened and the rain poured down.

"We're not getting over any rivers for some time," said Tom, looking at the torrent.

While we were waiting for the weather to improve, we fell in with Mr. Cameron, who had a sheep station at [20]Kakahu.

---

20   Twenty miles from Timaru.

Shipwrecks and Bush Felling

Once the ladies were settled, we went back to our work.

"I want to build a woolshed and a cottage," he said, "would you do some work for me? My two sisters are on their way to New Zealand."

G.R. Meredith / W.E. Hamilton

"I can't. I'm on my way to meet my family who are arriving on the Jane Fletcher," I said, "and after that we are going back to Waimate to continue cutting timber for Mr. Studholme."

"You won't get through to Lyttleton in this weather," said Mr. Cameron, "and even when the rain stops, it could be weeks before the rivers are low enough to ford. Come with me and at least make a start on the work."

"But we don't have our tent or gear with us," said Tom, "we left them at Waimate."

"I have a few tools you can use," said Mr. Cameron, "and a tarpaulin. You can shelter under it until you knock together a hut."

At last he persuaded us to join him, so we followed him to a very rugged piece of bush. It was rough building a hut in the pouring rain with less than ideal tools. We had to camp on the wet ground for a week with only the tarpaulin over us at night. But once we got a roof over our heads, we started cutting timber for the woolshed and cottage. While we were doing this, Cameron heard his sisters were at Lyttleton waiting to join him. So, he set off to meet them in a Bullock drag. On his return he gave me a large round tent which he had bought and said:

"Fix this up for my sisters as best you can, George, I need to keep my eye on the bullocks. They are black and if they stray into the bush, I will never find them again."

"You should have left your sisters with Mrs. Rogers at Levels station until we have the cottage ready for them, Boss," I said.

"I tried to, George, but they refused to stay and insisted on coming along with me. They say they are quite prepared to

Shipwrecks and Bush Felling

rough it."

"Yes, but this is exceptionally rough, even for New Zealand bush conditions."

"I know, just do the best you can."

So, it fell to me to make the two ladies as comfortable as possible under the circumstances. No easy matter without the necessary tools. Nevertheless, I picked out a well sheltered grassy spot and had the tent up and firmly pegged down by nightfall. In addition, I made some makeshift bunks and a table and chairs. While I was busy, Cameron came along and peeked inside to see how I was getting on.

"Come here, Maryanne and Sophia," he called, "have a look at New Zealand life."

"It's Robinson Crusoe's house," they laughed, greatly amused.

"It's very rough," I said, "but tomorrow I promise to make the beds softer."

Then I carried their boxes into the tent and left them to unpack while I started a campfire outside. And that took their fancy even more than the tent did. Once the young ladies were settled, Tom and I went back to our regular work and got on so well with the woolshed it was ready for the shearing.

"Give me a hand with the shearing while the weather's good and the wool is dry," said Mr. Cameron, "and you can work on the cottage on wet days."

We agreed and in this way we eventually got one room of the cottage in good order. Then before we had finished shearing, and with the kitchen half-finished, the young ladies took over these apartments.

G.R. Meredith / W.E. Hamilton

Shin Plasters

Once the floodwaters had gone down, Tom and I were anxious to get our job finished and away to Lyttleton, for we were three months delayed. Mr. Cameron gave us a cheque of seventy-five pounds each (the biggest sum I had ever made) and we set off once more.

There was very little money in circulation in 1859. The way the problem was got around was Captain Cain issued 'notes in hand,' which answered capitally at the time. Life was good and our pockets were full of I.O.Us. In this happy state of mind, we wandered into the store to swap some of them into cash.

"Will you cash these?" I said to Captain Cain, pulling a fistful of promissory notes out of my pocket.

"No boys, hold on to them. Just get any stores you need and we'll settle up later."

"Why?" I asked.

"Well, we're in a bit of a muddle," said Captain Cain. "Barnes the mailman was taking seventy I.O.Us to Christchurch

Shipwrecks and Bush Felling

when he capsized in the Rangitata River. They all went out to sea, so everyone who has them needs to get them exchanged at the bank."

While we were talking, the steamer The Lucky Jane from Sydney arrived with stores for Captain Cain.

"I'm looking for a couple of men," said Yanky Sam, coming in the store. "You blokes are sailors, do you want a job?"

"What do you want done?"

"There is no boat crew in Timaru, and the steamer needs unloading. If you help man my whaleboat there is ten shillings a day and plenty of beer for you."

That sounded good to us, so we agreed. Tom and I, a bloke named Bill, and a few other men ran the whaling boat into the surf and jumped in. We rowed out to the ship and started ferrying cargo to the shore. All went well until the last boatload. The rolling heavy seas were getting rough and it took us all our time to hold her. However, we got alongside the vessel and I loaded up. Then away we went using our oars in real sailor fashion as we could see the seas getting higher.

"This will be a rough landing," I said.

"It certainly will," said Tom, "we will be lucky if we get to the shore without being tipped over." Fortunately, we managed to land high and dry on the beach and after making the boat fast, we headed to the hotel to change our clothes. While we were walking, we noticed a stream of blood behind us, and found that Bill (having struck a broken bottle when jumping out of the boat) had cut the calf of his leg. We were troubled about it, for it was bleeding badly. When we got to the hotel, we opened our swags and cut the tail off a shirt.

"This is worse than I thought," said Tom, when he further

examined the cut and bound it up with the impromptu bandage. "Perhaps we can get some sticking plaster at the store."

As luck would have it, Captain Cain didn't have any. The next day I bathed Bill's leg with warm water, washed the rag and placed it back on the wound. Poor Bill's leg was getting more painful, so I went to the pub to get some brandy.

"Here will you take an I.O.U?" I asked Yanky Sam. I pulled a note out of my pocket.

To my surprise, I found I had taken two out, and they were firmly stuck together. When I peeled them apart, I saw there was some kind of sticky stuff on the back of them.

I believe one of these would make a good plaster for Bill's leg, I thought.

"Hey, you chaps," I called out. When I had their attention, I showed them how the I.O.U notes stuck together. "One of these might make a good plaster for Bill's leg," I said.

"There's no harm in giving it a trial," they said, nodding their heads.

I took the rag off Bill's leg again. Then I washed the sore with hot water and wiped it well around the cut. Tom made the I.O.U warm by holding it over a billy of boiling water. Everybody watched intently as I smoothed it over the cut, where it stuck like a leech. Before an hour had passed Bill said it did not feel painful and the next morning, he was able to walk about. The plaster continued to stick fast, and every day Bill's leg improved. Now the worry was over, we had heaps of fun.

"You're worth a pound so long as you keep your plaster on," we teased.

After a week of chaffing, Bill was keen to be rid of his

Shipwrecks and Bush Felling

I.O.U-a-pound plaster.

"Get it off me, George," he begged, "my leg feels much better now and I can't stand any more jokes."

"Oh, all right, Bill," I said.

So, the next night when we were all sitting around the fire with the billy boiling, I held Bill's leg over the steam. Then starting with one corner of the note, I carefully peeled it off. It took some time to get it completely removed because I didn't want to start his leg bleeding again. But patience will always succeed, and in half an hour I had it off without any pain to Bill. Bill fairly hugged me when he saw the healed cut, and the other chaps too were delighted with the success of the I.O.U plaster.

"Come on," I said, waving it, "lets trade this plaster in for drinks all round."

I got a bottle of brandy and handed the note to old Sam, thinking he would refuse it, but he didn't, he just put it in the box. The news spread, and after that, I.O.U's were called shin-plasters, right up to the time they were replaced with proper currency.

G.R. Meredith / W.E. Hamilton

Bridge Building

Once again, Tom and I set out for Lyttleton and once again our luck was out, for we had to stop at Rhodes Station for the night.

"Just the two men I want to see," said [21]Rhodes, "I want you to erect a bridge on the Timaru road over Bad Creek."

"Do you mean the spot where all the bullock drivers get stuck when they're carting wood to Timaru?"

"That's the place."

"We can't," I said, "I'm going to meet my parents in Lyttleton and Tom is meeting his sweetheart. Already we are three months late."

"What's more, we don't have our gear with us," said Tom, "we left it at Waimate because we haven't finished that job yet."

---

21 Robert Heaton Rhodes was the biggest carter of wool in the district and the founder of the New Zealand Shipping Company 'The Kaiapoi Woolen Co.'

Shipwrecks and Bush Felling

"I want you to erect a bridge over Bad Creek."

"The bullock driver can take you to Captain Cain's store for tools and stores," said Rhodes. "You don't even have to cut the trees down. Crabbe the Maori is felling the trees and my bullock drivers will cart them about for you. I pay you well," he added persuasively.

Now we were in a fix to know what to do. I had a private talk with Tom and we decided to quote him a big price, as we were keen to get to Lyttleton. But as luck would have it, when we gave in our price, Rhodes said:

"Alright, start in the morning and I'll give you an order for the Captain to get your tools and supplies."

So once again a tempting job hindered us from getting away as we had wished. With help from the bullock driver who carried the stores for the station, we got the bridge finished in four weeks.

"That is mighty fine work," said Rhodes, handing us thirty-six pounds each.

The day the bridge was opened, there were six loaded drays of wool eager to cross. While we were packing up our camp, we noticed two bullock drivers with loaded drays on the bridge at once.

"That is quite enough weight for a new bridge," I said to Tom.

"Here comes another, and it looks like he's not going to wait for the others to get off," said Tom in alarm.

"Stop," I shouted, running towards the driver, "wait until the others are off the bridge, three are too many for safety."

The driver did not take my warning too kindly. He made for me with his whip, but I pulled it away from him and threw it into the creek. Then I took off my coat and gave him a good thrashing, for I had not been at sea for nine years without learning something about self-defense. After that little incident, only one dray crossed at a time and I had no further trouble.

Shipwrecks and Bush Felling

The Last of my Single Years

Finally, Tom and I were on our way to Lyttleton. At Timaru we collected our cheques for the work we did for Levels station. We got as far as Arawanui bush the first night, and forty-eight hours later we were in Christchurch exhausted.

"As much as I want to see Mary Anne, I can't face trekking up the Port Hills without a couple of days rest," said Tom, as we made camp.

"Me too," I said, "I'm dead beat."

We had to have two days rest before going to Lyttleton, and when I got to my mother's cottage I was very relieved. My family gave me a warm welcome.

"Oh, George, it is so good to see you," said my mother kissing me.

"It certainly is," said my dear old dad.

"This is my good friend and fellow bush sawyer, Tom."

"Welcome, Tom," said my parents.

"Thomas, I hardly recognize you," I said, as my brother

walked into the room.

"Hello George," he said, clapping me on the back.

"How did you like your sea voyage?" I asked.

"I think I'd rather be a bush sawyer than a sailor," said Thomas. "Storms at sea are better kept as stories."

We all laughed.

Lyttleton with the Sumner road winding around the hills.

"What do you think of New Zealand, Dad?"

"It's a grand land Son," said my father, easing himself into a chair by the fire. Fresh air, magnificent scenery, and not crowded like London."

"I'm sorry I took so long to get here, the weather and unexpected work held me up."

"We got your letters, so we weren't worried," said my father.

"I've got a big job down in Waimate to finish, but when that is done, I'll rent a cottage in Timaru and you can come and

Shipwrecks and Bush Felling

live with me."

"That would be wonderful," said Dad.

All the time we were talking, my mother was peeling potatoes and preparing dinner.

"Come and have something to eat," she said, taking a pot of stew off the fire.

We had a good tea together and then Tom left. Three weeks later he was back.

"I'm getting married at the end of the week," he said.

"Congratulations."

"Will you be my best man, George?"

"Of course."

So, Tom married eighteen-year-old Mary Anne Reecks on the tenth of March 1857. About a week after his marriage we got a letter from Studholme begging us to come back to Waimate to finish our contract.

'The stack of timber you left is all gone and we urgently need more,' he wrote.

We were keen to go, the trouble was to get back again as it was unreasonable to expect Tom's new wife to walk the whole way. In the end I brought a strong horse and Tom and his wife caught a lift with Barnes the mailman. The postal service turned out to be a slow way to travel. I managed to get to Wiamate a week before they did as they got stuck at the big rivers for five days. Mr. Studholme was so anxious for us to get started, he sent two saddled horses to Timaru for Tom and his wife. While we waited for them, I got a Maori man called Solomon to help me fell and cut logs ready for sawing. When Tom and his wife arrived, he and I got straight into the sawing. Before long, the timber was stacking up and Studholme was pleased with our progress.

But things were not going so well for Tom's wife. She missed her folks and at the end of eight months roughing it in the bush was not well. When we finished the contract, Tom said:

My mother was peeling potatoes.

"This is not working out. I'm going to have to call it quits, George. Mary Anne is ill and homesick."

"I'll be sorry to see you go, Tom," I said, "but I can see it is

Shipwrecks and Bush Felling

the right thing. What are you going to do?"

"I'll take Mary Anne back to Lyttleton so she can be near her mother, and I'll pick up some work there."

Because I could see there was little chance of Tom coming back, I paid him for his half of the land at Champion Station and took the lot. Then we packed up and headed off to Timaru. When we got there, the Sydney ship the Lucky Jane was in the harbour. She was taking in wool bound for Lyttleton.

"Take this to my parents," I said to Tom, as he and Mary Anne boarded the vessel. "It's a letter telling of all my adventures and explaining the delay in getting up to see them. I'm hoping my brother Thomas might take up pit-sawing and join me."

"I'll make sure they get it," said Tom.

As I waved them goodbye, I was very sorry to see Tom go, for he was a fine fellow and we got on well.

A letter came back with postman Barnes. Much to my disappointment, Thomas was shepherding sheep for Mr. Rhodes at Levels Station. I got Joe Adams (a sailor) instead. He was a very awkward man and I had a lot of trouble with him, for he was bad-tempered. However, we rubbed along the best we could. It took a big job, cutting timber for an accommodation house on the bank of the Waitaki River, to break down his barriers. Another team of sawyers were working alongside us. We helped one another in our work and made big money. On Sundays the four of us got together to play cards and eventually we became good friends. Over time Joe improved beyond recognition and became quite a good pitman, working with me until August 1859, when he left me at Timaru to go shearing.

G.R. Meredith / W.E. Hamilton

Marriage

At the beginning of 1859, the township of Timaru consisted of six houses, a store, and Robert Rhodes two sheds. But with the arrival of the [22]Strathallan on January the twenty-first, the town was rapidly growing. By September of the same year I decided to bring my parents to live in Timaru as I had made a deal with Mr. Persimmon to lease a little cottage from him. Then I saddled up my horse and set off for Lyttleton.

As if the weather knew I was on my way, the skies opened and rain pelted down as I rode. The going was rough and fording swollen rivers was risky. But fortunately, I had a good horse under me, and he got me safely through them all. After staying with my parents for a month, an immigrant ship called the Creswell came to Lyttleton on the twelfth of September 1859.

"I suppose you are going down to the docks like all the young fellows," said my father, noticing me brushing my hair

---

22   The first passenger ship.

Shipwrecks and Bush Felling

and shining up my hobnail boots.

"Of course, there might be some pretty young girls aboard."

"You're twenty-five, high time you found a wife and settled down," said my mother.

"It's hard to do that," I said pulling a face, "there's a big shortage of girls and they are snatched up and married within a few weeks of getting off the boat."

"Well, you'll just have to be quick at making up your mind if you see one you fancy," said my dear old dad.

I whistled as I strode to the dock. When I got there, the passengers were about to disembark. I jostled my way through the crowd of young men, and noticed a girl and her older sister coming down the gangplank. The older sister was pretty and it was love at first sight with me. As luck would have it, the younger girl was looking for a box.

Lyttleton again
From the Illustrated London News 1863.

G.R. Meredith / W.E. Hamilton

"Can I help you?"

"Can I help you?" I asked, seizing my opportunity.
"I've lost my box, it's a brown one with the name Mary Ferguson on it."

Shipwrecks and Bush Felling

"I'll look for it and bring it to you when I find it," I said. "Where are you staying?"

"That's very kind, my family and I are staying in the barracks,"

As I watched the Ferguson family walk away, I resolved there and then, to win and marry the older sister. I searched about and at last found the box which I hoisted onto my back and carried to the barracks. Mary seeing me walk down the path with her box, came to the gate and thanked me for my assistance.

"You come from a big family," I said, smoothing the way for the big question. "How many brothers and sisters do you have?"

"There are twelve of us," said Mary. "There is my older sister Jessie who is twenty-one, and then James and me. I'm one year older than Catherine who is fifteen, and then there is Alexander, Jane, Ellen, Christina and Margret. The toddlers are Susan and my nephew James, and the baby is Alice. My oldest sister Anne didn't come." [23]

"I'm George Meredith and I'd like to meet Jessie," I said. Then I slid in the big question. "Would you introduce me to her?"

"Sure."

She called Jessie out and we struck up a conversation where I discovered the family had come from Edinburgh, that Mr. Ferguson was a schoolmaster, and he intended to start a private school. The encounter left me even more determined to marry Jessie, and I saw no reason to muck around so I got straight to the point.

---

23   In 1861 Athol was born.

G.R. Meredith / W.E. Hamilton

"I am a pit-sawyer," I said, "I have a hundred-acres in Champion Station, the demand for timber is huge so I make big money, and I have leased a cottage in Timaru. I'd like to ask your father if I can marry you."

Jessie was not opposed to the idea, so she called her father and we discussed the matter. He objected for a few hours and raised many difficulties, but I overcame them and Jessie and I got married. Even for those days, the courtship was considered quick. Our story made the papers. The Lyttleton Times reporting on the arrival of the Cresswell on September the seventeenth 1859 wrote:

'One young woman who landed on Tuesday was met on the landing by a well-to-do young swain who offered her a home, wooed her on the spot and married her the next morning.'

The old saying 'marry in haste repent at leisure,' was not so with us. Jessie turned out to be a very good wife and is still with me fifty-six years later.

Shipwrecks and Bush Felling

Married Life

There was more work further down country, and I wanted to get my parents settled in the cottage I had leased for them. So, taking my new wife with me, the four of us boarded the Lady Jane bound for Timaru carrying stores for Le Crene, Campbell, and Rhodes. It was a rough passage and an equally rough landing, for there was no harbour or breakwater, just the open beach. We had to land in a whaleboat and wait for the sea to run the boat up on the beach. I wondered how Jessie would manage; but a woman adventurous enough to marry a fellow after a day's courtship, was well up to it.

"I'm looking forward to a nice cup of tea," said my mother as we traipsed up the beach.

"You shall have one as soon as we get home," I said.

But when I went to get the key for the cottage, I found Mr. Persimmon had not honoured our agreement. He had sold the cottage and left the district. Now I was in an awkward fix, for though I had hoped to bring my father and mother with me, I did not think of bringing a wife. Moreover, the promise of a comfortable home was part of my marriage proposal. To make matters worse, there was a great shortage of housing. Moreover, a shipload of passengers had that very morning disembarked from the Strathallan. Many people were living in tents as they waited for timber to build their houses.

Mr. Rhodes of Levels Station turned his woolshed into a barracks which many preferred to living under canvas. Little did I think when I and Tom were cutting timber for this building, that one day I would be sheltering in it with my wife and parents. We made our way over to the barracks, and I went up two or three bales and selected the top of two bales for Jessie and me, while my parents chose another two bales. Then we fixed up shawls and blankets as screens and made ourselves as comfortable as we could.

A soon as it was possible to obtain timber, I built a good house in Timaru of three rooms; a bedroom at either end and a large kitchen in the middle with a double chimney in the centre. Now that my wife and parents were comfortably settled, and feeling the responsibility to support a family, I was keen to get away and to make more big cheques (for sawyers were in huge demand in all bushes.) I was offered a large order in the Arawhanui bush, and Jessie's brother James Ferguson agreed to join me as a sawing partner.

"I will get home every weekend, Jessie," I promised, "if weather permits."

"George, I want to come with you and James," she said.

"But bush life is no life for a woman," I said, remembering Tom's wife Mary Anne. "It's a rough life."

"I don't care, I don't even mind living in a tent," she said, "please take me with you, George."

Shipwrecks and Bush Felling

She was very hard to resist, so at last I agreed to let her come. We packed a few things, saddled up and rode twelve miles to the Arawhanui bush. As we rode into the camp, I remembered Tom's wife's reaction to bush life.

"Do you regret coming?" I asked Jessie.

But My wife was made of sterner stuff than Mary Anne.

"Not at all," she assured me.

We set up our tent and after a few weeks I had a cosy hut built. We were now comfortable and happy. But the demand for timber was so great, James and I could scarcely find time to eat meals. I had not been more than three months in the bush when another station holder came to see me.

"When you are finished here, George, come and cut timber in my bush in Waihi. I want enough to build a large house and a woolshed," said Mr. Mc Donald.

"That's a new bush," I said, "there are no huts there and it will take a bit of time to get set up, which means a lot of work before we make any money."

"I'll pay you eight hundred pounds for the job."

Eight-hundred pounds was a lot of money in those days, so I agreed to come to him as soon as I had finished my present orders.

My wife was pleased with the location as it was not far from Geraldine where her sister (now married to William Young) lived. Jessie stayed with them while I was getting fixed up in the bush, for she was expecting our first child. When we got the mill and the bark hut built, my wife joined me again, and the [24]Waihi bush became our home for some years to come. During that time, George was born, and in 1862 two years

---

24   Later known as Woodbury.

later, our second child, Catherine Anne, arrived.

By now my parents had shifted to Geraldine, twelve miles away. In addition, my wife's father, Daniel Fergusson (after teaching in Kaiapoi for two years) had shifted to Temuka and built the first private school there.

Daniel Fergusson was a clever man, much loved and respected by all who came in contact with him. He had studied at St. Andrews University in Fife in Scotland and had a passion for languages and poetry, which he composed in English, Scots and Gaelic.

"After he won the Queen's prize of nine pounds, three years in succession, other Highlanders would not compete against him, and the Gaelic Society banned him from further competitions," said Jessie laughing, "though they did pay him eleven pounds to translate his final prize poem from Gaelic into English."

With two children and another one on the way, we needed something more substantial than the bark hut. When the order for Mr. McDonald's house was finished, we set about building a nice cottage near my work. When it was done, I felt well set up, for I already had a good horse and once I got a buggy and harness, we were able to get out on Sundays to visit relatives who lived quite handy.

My next job was to cut timber for Mr. Cox to build the Church of England in Geraldine. Since he wanted it built of [25]Kahikatea and there was not any in the Waihi bush, I shifted to a bush called Fairfield about seven miles from his station. As there was a good house close by, we were soon comfortably settled.

---

25   White pine.

Shipwrecks and Bush Felling

Jessie and Catherine Anne.

G.R. Meredith / W.E. Hamilton

Once again, as Jim and I undulated our way along logs with our saw, the planks stacked up. We had only just completed the work for the church when another large order came from the overseer of Four Peaks station.

"I'm after timber for fencing," he said.

"Alright, I don't mind splitting posts," I said, for a change suited me and the money was still good.

So, we worked hard splitting posts for three years. Towards the end of that time, a sawmill, started cutting timber in the Rekapuka bush near Geraldine. When I saw what it could produce, I knew we were finished.

"Pit-sawing has had its day, James," I said. "We can't compete with that mill, we'd best hang up our saws and look for something else to do."

So, I turned my face away from the bush, and with the whining sing of the sawmill blowing in the breeze, I became a farmer. I farmed the land for a few years and grew some wonderful crops, but I didn't take to it as much as bush life.

Shipwrecks and Bush Felling

Lime Burning

The news was spreading of gold being found in the Kakahu river, so James and I set off to investigate. In the the river, I made a big find.

"Look at this James," I said, picking up a piece of gold.

"Wow," said James, "it's as big as a pen!"

That chunk of gold spurred us on to start hunting in earnest. But alas, we prospected for about two weeks finding coal, iron, and marble, but no gold. In the end we gave it up as a bad job and started for home. On the way I was very much taken with a pretty spot for a house and later bought twenty-five acres of it.

Our need for a bigger house was increasing as every year or two another baby was born. By 1868 Athol Richard, Jessie, and Marion, had joined our family and we were bursting out of our little cottage. That was a tumultuous year, some of it good and some of it bad. I built a cottage, my mother died, Christina was born, and there was a huge flood and fire. Christina's birth was good and the new cottage of four rooms was good. But just as we had everything finished and in order, along came the big flood which almost swept us away. We fared better than our neighbours, however, in that we kept the house, but we lost all the fences.

I had a family of eight to support. The farm brought in a bit and I was able to grow all our vegetables, but I missed the big money of pit-sawing. Shortly after the flood, I discovered plenty of coal on my property and decided to make a few adjustments to our fireplace so we could burn coal. I pulled out the chimney stones, put them in a bucket and carried them outside. Then I cleaned up the fireplace and made it ready for more iron bars. While I was in my workshop fixing up the iron grate, my wife called:

"Come and have a look at this, George." She pointed to the smoking bucket of stones. "That's lime, the same as I've seen in the old country."

I got a stick and poked at it. It felt like flour and was white.

"You're right," I said. "We could do something with this. We have tons and tons of this stone on our land and plenty of coal handy."

Shipwrecks and Bush Felling

I decided to make adjustments to our fireplace.

G.R. Meredith / W.E. Hamilton

So, I harnessed the horse and drove into Temuka and Geraldine to consult the bricklayers.

"Build a kiln and burn away as fast as you can," they said.

That was the end of farming for a living. Everything was put aside for the new venture of lime burning, I built a brick kiln shaped like a stumpy round tower with a small arched opening at the bottom. To fire the kiln, I first put in a layer of wood, a barrow load of coal was spread over the wood, and three barrows of limestone chips were tipped on top of the coal. This was repeated until the kiln was full. Then I fired it from a narrow gap at the bottom.

At the end of the firing, the powdered lime fell through the gap, and was shovelled out the arched opening.

The old saying 'every cloud has a silver lining' proved true for us, when in December the disastrous fire swept through Timaru. Thirty -six buildings burnt to the ground. Those who lost buildings were keen to replace wooden structures with brick ones, and there was a big demand for lime. I was well prepared, and my lime shed was full to the top when the large orders came in. I was so busy I had two teams of horses carting bags of lime to Timaru. By now, George was twelve and Athol was nine, so I put them in charge of a team each. My eldest son George was a wonderful lad with horses, and had his team so well trained he did not need reigns. They were very fond of him and would follow him almost anywhere. He could get them to do anything by just speaking to them as if they were human beings.

One day he was carting lime when a policeman stopped him.

"What's the meaning of this?" said the policeman, "It is

Shipwrecks and Bush Felling

illegal to drive without reigns."

"Please, Sir, they don't need them," said George.

"What do you mean they don't need them? They might run away and crash into someone."

"No, they won't, they will do whatever I want them to. They will even turn a circle if I tell them too. But I'm sorry for breaking the law. I'll pay the fine."

By now quite a crowd had gathered. The police and onlookers were amused to hear this statement and were keen for him to prove his words.

"I'll make a deal with you, Son," said the policeman. "If you can get those horses to turn a circle, I'll let you off."

"Thank you, Sir."

"Star and Bessy, turn a circle," said George. Obediently the horses pulled the cart around in a complete circle, much to the on-lookers astonishment. Those animals would do anything for him, and he was very caring of them. No matter how tired he was at the end of a long day, he always fed and rubbed down his horses before he came in for his much-needed meal.

Sales slackened once Timaru had recovered from the big fire. When my shed was full of lime ready for emergency orders, I got road-making contracts for myself, my two teams, George and Athol. Now we had a lime burning business and a road-making business. This kept us busy for the two years before the railway work started.

G.R. Meredith / W.E. Hamilton

Railway Work

In 1870 Captain Cain became the Mayor of Timaru. In the following year work started on the railway line. I hitched up the horses and we all went to a big opening ceremony. After a speech, Captain Cain's wife turned the first sod and we all clapped and cheered; for the railway line would bring in much work. Already the railway contractor Mr. B.G. Wright wanted six thousand posts and ten thousand nails, as he was fencing both sides of the proposed line from Pleasant Point to Fairlie's Bush. I won the tender to both provide the posts and deliver them and the nails to Pleasant Point. To do this, I leased twenty acres of bush in Kakahu from Mr. John Hay, who was a farmer and a gentleman.

"If things go as well as I hope," I said to Jessie, "I'll build a bigger house. For by now, our four-roomed-cottage was too small for us.

As I hoped, I did well out of this contract. I kept my promise to my wife and hired a stonemason to build a large house at Rocky Point from the stone on my property.

Shipwrecks and Bush Felling

"See if you can get better coal for the house."

G.R. Meredith / W.E. Hamilton

In between felling and carting posts and nails to Pleasant Point, I did the carpentry on the house. It was a good house when it was finished and my dear old dad got to see it before he died in 1873. We lived at Rocky Point for forty-three years and the rest of our children, Eva, Alice, James, Eliza, Charles, Samuel Earnest, William Edward, and John Thomas, were born there.

My next job was to act as the agent for Mr. Wright, who was in charge of a large contract for crates to keep the Rangitata river in its proper course. He gave me ten shillings a day and paid all my travelling expenses. I had to go from bush to bush to get the necessary spars. This was no easy matter as some of the spars had to be twenty feet long. Moreover, the butt was to be twenty inches, tapering all the way down to twelve inches at the top. Trunks like that were not easy to find, but I got all I needed at the Waihi bush. Mr. Wright was so pleased with my work he gave me a carting contract, which meant my two sons had work again. In addition to transporting the timber, we carted boulders to fill between the cracks as the crates were being made. It was a long job and good-paying one for all concerned.

By 1874 the railway was making a start on the Christchurch line, and the Government was pushing to get it done. Now there was a big demand for railway sleepers. So, after finishing the crate job, I decided it was time to tackle sawmilling. I was pleased to be back in my old bush where I had forty acres of good black pine and totara trees.

I rigged up a portable sawmill[26] under an open-sided shed

---

26   George did not describe his mill. This description is based on the most common type of sawmills of the time.

Shipwrecks and Bush Felling

with a corrugated iron roof. The mill consisted of twin circular saws; one of which was mounted in a bench of wooden rollers, while the other was suspended directly above, and overlapped slightly. It made a fearsome noise as I pushed the logs through the saws and James tailed them out the other side. We started taking orders from the Geraldine and the Timaru Road Boards, and this work kept my saws spinning until the railway got well along the Canterbury plains.

Fortunately, as demand for timber was slowing, they started building the Timaru hospital in stone. So, once again there was a big demand for lime. I went back to my old job of lime burning and I got a contract to supply and cart seven-hundred bags of lime to the hospital building site. It was very tiring work. I worked long hours night and day as the kiln had to be fed constantly, and I was the only one to do it. From time to time the demand was greater than I could supply, and I could not burn it fast enough. It was almost a relief when orders got slack. In slack times I took advantage of the spell to get the shed filled with lime ready for the next rush.

I was prospering. I had a nice house, a wonderful family and a comfortable home life. I had extended family nearby, and farmers wanted lime for manure. But just when things were looking bright, Mr. Landown of Christchurch formed a company and built a large kiln just above my small homemade kiln. It was called the Hogburn Kiln and cost one-thousand-and-eight-hundred pounds. Since Landown was operating on a much bigger scale than me, and employed a great number of men, I felt sure they would soon outdo me in production.

"That's the end of burning lime," I said to Jessie, the day the Hogburn Kiln fired up. "Tomorrow I go back to saw-milling.

G.R. Meredith / W.E. Hamilton

The farmers are upgrading their huts to houses and there is a big demand for timber again."

It would have been better for me if I'd stuck to lime burning for there was good money in it and the Hogburn Kiln did not turn out a success. Their lime wasn't any good as the lumps of stone they put in the kiln were too large and not sufficiently burned. Landown built a hotter kiln, thinking it would burn better that way. But the process was slow and he was losing money. In the end, the company chucked it and the one-thousand-eight-hundred-pound kiln lay idle for years. Eventually the property was bought by Mr. Griffiths who pulled it down and sold the bricks at a hundred bricks for three shillings. It is a pity I shut down my kiln for if I had kept going, I would have picked up the unfulfilled orders when the company broke up.

Instead, I moved from bush to bush with my mill, scratching out a living. Things changed when the railway got well into the Timaru hills, for then there was a great need for horse teams. George, though still a lad, was as good as any man with horses, and I had two first-class teams, my favourite horse Star, amongst them. George and I got work on the Timaru-cutting at three and ten shillings a day. Our job was to cart lime into the cutting on the trip there, and cart clay out of the cutting on the trip back. We kept at this job until it was finished and made good money. Moreover, since I grew my own feed for the horses, it left a big cheque at the end of each month. (The saving on feed was especially big because oats were five shillings a bushel at that time.)

Shipwrecks and Bush Felling

Coal

When the railway work finished, I worked at home for some time putting things in order once more.

"The farmers are needing more lime," I said to Jessie one day, "perhaps it is time to fire up the old kiln again."

"That's a good idea, George," she said. "Do you have enough coal in the shed?"

"No, I need to go and get a good amount before I make a start."

"See if you can get some better coal for the house while you're at it," said my wife, poking the fire, "this stuff stinks of sulphur."

I hitched the horse to the cart, took my spade and pickaxe, and set off to my coal patch. I started loading the cart with the poor-quality coal (for it was only three foot below the surface and suitable for lime burning.) All the time I was digging, I kept my eye open for better coal. I had to go through a five-foot seam of poor coal, and then a further twelve-foot seam of better coal, before I found a three-foot seam of quality coal which built up my hopes. These three seams all led into a fifty-foot hill nearby. I loaded my wagon with plenty of coal for the household and lime burning, and I should have been content with this. But I was very excited and ended up risking more than I should have.

"I'm convinced there is quality coal in that hill out the back," I said to my wife, as I replenished the fire with better coal.

"It does smell better," said Jessie.

"And further down, there is even better stuff. If we mined it properly, we could make a fortune."

"Yes, but George, that would cost lots of money,"

"I could find investors," I said.

In hindsight, I should have left it alone.

When I let my discovery be known, a party of men from Timaru floated a company and made me an offer.

The house at Rock Point.

Shipwrecks and Bush Felling

"If you can strike a five-foot seam of good coal, George, we will lease the section from you on your own terms."

So down into the ground I went. I was not more than six-foot from the eight-foot seam when I came upon a seam of white drift sand, which rushed on me as fast as I could shovel it out. I then made a box the size of the shaft, stationed two men at the top with a winch, and went down again. But even then, it fell in faster than the men could winch it up. And since I was paying them ten shillings a day for eight hours of work, I quickly abandoned the idea.

"I'll get a strong pump made," I said to Jessie. "There is a firm in Christchurch that can make a pump to lift six-hundred gallons an hour."

It might have worked, but my luck ran out again, for before the pump was half-finished, the firm went bung and it never reached me. This finished me, for my funds were getting low and I could see many expenses and no profit before me.

"I'm calling it quits," I said to Jessie, "tomorrow I will start lime burning again, which is what I should have done in the first place."

I fired up the kiln and filled my shed with two-hundred bags of lime. As for the shaft, it is still there and coal as well. All it needs is the necessary pumps to keep the water down, and I am confident to this day that it could be worked and money made out of it, but it won't be me who does it.

G.R. Meredith / W.E. Hamilton

Milling Again

Business was slow and orders for the lime only trickled in. The farmers could not use as much lime as I could make, so I stockpiled enough for local orders and went back to sawmilling in my old bush at Waihi. Over the next five years I shifted my mill five times as I went from bush to bush cutting timber. The last shift was to Geraldine on the Government Reserve, where I cut the timber lying about the ground for the Geraldine Road Board. That was the last cutting I did in the South Island. I bought my plant home again and continued farming. After getting my crops in, I took a contract for road making. I didn't make much out of that job, however, as the weather was against us and my horses had to be fed whether working or playing. Nevertheless, I carried on until 1895.

My children by now were all grown and many were married. Some still lived nearby, but others were scattered as far as the North Island. One day I got a letter from Athol.

Shipwrecks and Bush Felling

'I've got a government contract for a bridge at [27]Strathmore,' he wrote. Bring the mill and I will pay all your expenses to get it here, plus seven pounds a month and two shillings per hundred logs of timber cut. Don't bother to bring the engine, I don't need it. But hurry because we have no time to lose.'

Thinking it was a fair proposition, I wrote back:

'Yes, I can come and will bring the mill with me. But only on the condition I am the manager as I am past the age of being ordered about by anyone, and feel my long experience in the bush entitles me to the claim.'

Athol agreed to my terms, so I packed up my plant and had it delivered to Stratford by boat and train. As I travelled up the country and sailed across to the North Island, the weather turned foul and the rain poured down in torrents.

My daughter Jessie was now Mrs. Kennedy and lived in Toko fifteen miles from Stratford. I stayed with her, and Athol and I worked there for about three weeks while we waited for the floods to recede. When the road got passable, we loaded our tools and tent behind our saddles, and rode to the bush.

This turned out to be the toughest job I ever tackled.

"Talk about not being able to see the wood for the trees," I said, when I saw our destination.

The land was so thick with heavy timber and dense scrub we had to go into the bush on our hands and knees; all in the pouring rain. "There is no way we can set up the mill and start working while we are hemmed in like this," I said to Athol, as

---

27   About twenty miles from Stratford in the Taranaki district.

we crawled through pig fern and [28]pongas, "we'll have to burn out a clearing.

Getting a fire started under such wet conditions was almost impossible. But the weather eased slightly, and in a gap between showers we got the bush alight. It was a slow burn, however.

"We'll have to burn all night to make a clearing for tomorrow," I said.

We did not get much rest that night. The rain fell on our heads and the smouldering smoke stung our eyes. Nevertheless, we managed to burn a pathway from our camp to the road.

"That's better," said Athol, "we can see a little, what about putting the mill over there, it looks like a flat area."

"That looks good to me," I said, "let's get another fire going."

It was rough work and long hours until we got a good clear space. Obtaining that space, however, was tough. We were jammed up with heavy timber and couldn't burn fast.

"Getting this gap in the bush makes setting up the mill seem like easy work in comparison," I said, when we at last finished.

"That's if we can ever get it from Toko," said Athol, "the roads will be thick mud by now."

As the days passed, my son's gloomy prediction looked more and more likely. We managed to get some of the plant moved, but while the roads remained barely passable, there was no hope of getting the engine. While we were waiting for the weather to improve, we rigged up our saw bench and felled trees to be ready with plenty of logs when it came. It was a month before we got it. During that time, the only way we

---

28   Tall tree ferns.

Shipwrecks and Bush Felling

could get stores was by pack bullocks as we could not use the drays. Fortunately, nothing lasts forever, even New Zealand rain. Finally, after three days of hard slogging with twelve bullocks, we got the engine in place. No time was lost now in cutting timber for our much-needed hut, for we were sick of the tents and no wonder in such dampness. Once the hut was up, we started milling in earnest. I worked there with my son Athol for three and a half years. By the end of that time he was well established as a saw-miller at Strathmore. Then I went back home.

About a month later, I got another letter from Athol.

'Could you come back for a few months, Dad,' he wrote, 'I've bought a thicknesser to plane the wood and I need your help to set it up as I am very busy with lots of orders.'

Of course, I agreed to go. While I was packing, I had an idea concerning two of my younger sons.

"I might have a look around for some bush while I'm up there," I said to my wife, "perhaps there might be an opportunity to get Sam and Will launched into saw-milling."

With this idea in mind, once I finished giving Athol a hand, I took a trip around the area. I saw some splendid timber, but the opportunity I was looking for happened in the most unlikely way. When I was on a train travelling from New Plymouth to Toko to see my daughter Jessie, I happened to be seated not far from a young man. What caught my eye was he was looking at a plan.

"Excuse me, Sir," I said. "My name is Meredith, and I can't help but notice you are looking at a bush section. Are you the owner, because it seems to me it is just what I am looking for?"

"Green's the name," he said, shaking my hand. "No, it's not mine yet, but I hope to swap a team of bullocks for it."

"I'm a miller," I said, "I'm looking for timber to mill?"

"It's no good for that for there are no roads to it," said Green, "but I can tell you where you can mill."

"Where?"

"Bush ten miles from New Plymouth. It belongs to my brother who would be glad to clear the section, and my father is needing timber for a milking shed to house forty cows."

He drew a map and gave me a note for his father. I thanked him, and once I had spent some time with my daughter, headed back to New Plymouth.

Mr. Green was a fine man to do business with. We came to satisfactory terms about the bush. With one eye on the weather and without my tools, I immediately set to work clearing a campsite. My first need was a hut, for I was determined to be well sheltered when the inevitable rain came. As I was all alone, I resorted to hand-sawing and dug a pit near to some handy logs that would make good lengths for the mill shed, for I thought I could use the shorter offcuts for the hut. I could not wield the saw without a mate, however, so I went into town and got a man for the pit. But he took no interest in his work, being too much of a townie. I put up with him until the cutting was done, then I paid him off and was glad to be rid of him. Then I wrote to my sons:

'Pack up the mill plant, Will and Sam, and get up here as soon as possible.'

Shipwrecks and Bush Felling

They came as I instructed and we worked together to set up a milling business. I helped them for three and a half years. And when they were established, I took my share of the mill and left my sons to make the best of it.

This finished the seven years I worked in the North Island, half with my eldest son Athol and half with my two younger sons. I received the greatest kindness from Mr. and Mrs. Green and family, and eventually two of my sons married two of their daughters, and very fine and capable women they were, making excellent wives for Sam and Will who by this time were settling down to bush life.

G.R. Meredith / W.E. Hamilton

Journey's End

I was pleased to leave the North Island and get back to Canterbury as I didn't like so much wet weather. Moreover, it was 1902 and I was getting along in years. I found plenty to do getting my old home straightened up after my long absence. I then built portable tool sheds for contractors, carpenters and smithies until I was age seventy-six and getting a bit shaky.

"It's time to leave the farm," I said to Jessie one day. "We are getting too old to manage it."

"We've had many good years here," said my wife, patting the stone wall of our house.

"And many ups and downs," I said.

"Yes. Right from the first day I met you, our life together has been an adventure, George."

"You have been a good wife and mother, Jessie. All our twelve children have turned out well, thanks to your guiding hand."

"I don't want to sell the old place," said Jessie,

Shipwrecks and Bush Felling

My devoted daughter.

"We don't have to," I said. "Kate wants us to live with her, so we can lease it out."

So, we rented out Rocky Point and I got a nice little cottage built on Kate's section. The cottage is where I now live. The sun is streaming through the window and I am surrounded with all the comfort, love, and care, this devoted daughter can lavish on me. How strange it is that I finish the story of my life not more than a mile from the spot where I first cut timber for Mr. Studholme. Mine has been a long and eventful life with many ups and downs, truly the lot of all men. Studholme's woolshed still stands, and I often walk past it. As I walk, I reflect on my

G.R. Meredith / W.E. Hamilton

life. Those early years at sea were filled with hardship, yet they were wonderful preparation for life in New Zealand. For this I am truly grateful, for I have liked my life in the Dominion better than England.

It is written in the Good Book 'he who finds a wife finds a good thing.' I found a good wife on the Lyttleton dock. She has been a wonderful mother to our family of six boys and six girls, and I thank God for his goodness that I have her with me still. I am sad to relate that my eldest son, George, my pal of long ago, died at age forty-seven. But the rest of the family are well, and a great comfort to us in our declining years. I'm still hale and hearty and able to potter about, but unfortunately, I am getting very deaf, which I find a great drawback. However, remembering that I am seventy-nine as I write, I am truly thankful to be as well as I am.

My father lived to be eighty-five, and I may reach that age yet. But whether I do or not, my life has been one adventure after another. If I had been born a few years earlier, I might have died of the plague in Shoreditch as many of my brothers and sisters did. And several times I nearly died at sea. But instead, I have lived at both ends of the world, and crisscrossed the sea between them. I am quite ready to meet my God and Savior, for I know He died for me, and I believe with all my heart that heaven will be the greatest adventure of all.

George Richard Meredith
1913

Shipwrecks and Bush Felling

Obituary
1/12/1918

One of Canterbury's fast disappearing band of Pioneers passed away in Waimate, in the person of Mr. George Meredith a member of an old Welsh family who arrived in Lyttleton in November 1854 and with the exception of one or two years spent in Taranaki, lived in Canterbury for sixty-four years.

He was one of the early settlers in Pleasant Valley, Geraldine. He was engaged in sawmilling for many years, and owned lime kilns and coal mines on his property at Kakahu.

The late Mr. Meredith made a large circle of friends, who deeply morn his death.

He is survived by his widow Jessie (daughter of the late Mr. Daniel Fergusson, at one time clerk to the court at Timaru) and five sons:

Athol (Strathmore)
Charles B.A.(Cambridge)
 Samuel (Ohura)
William (Ohura)

G.R. Meredith / W.E. Hamilton

John (Gore)
And six daughters:
Mrs Butcher (Waimate)
Mrs Kennedy (Tahora)
Dr. Eva M Clement (England)
Dr. Alice M Burn (England)
Miss Tina Meredith (Edinburgh)
Mrs. Heron (Geraldine)"

Shipwrecks and Bush Felling

Shipping Records
1/12/1918

George Richard Meredith's records compiled from the Lloyds Register by Ron Hawkins, retired Master Mariner

George Richard MEREDITH
b. 1st Sept. 1834
Crown St., Finchley, Shoreditch, London
Sea-going career: First ship; Only 11yrs old.

LONDON, of London, master Capt. Fraser, Barque, 239 tons, built Sunderland 1833. Owner: Master, M.Tait (L.R. 1844 Surveyed for a voyage from London to African coast.

A voyage to Sierra Leone to load logs which would then have been loaded at various ports along the coast. The outward-bound cargo would probable been 'Manchester Goods', textiles and manufactured products for trading.

Vessel was subsequently sold. (cf LR 1845/46)

G.R. Meredith / W.E. Hamilton

HERALD, Capt James. C. 1847

There are a number of possible HERALD's listed in Lloyd's Register. The most likely one is a 70 ton schooner built in the Scilly Isles in 1835. She was owned by Rodd & Co at the time and registered at Penzance. She was in the fruit trade, making voyages to the Mediterranean. I cannot find any record of a Capt. James being in command but Lloyd's Register shows Capt. Nance in command in 1850.

A voyage to St. Michaels, Western Isles (Azores) to load oranges. Signed on as boy wages £1 per month with 'bounty money' if vessel delivers first fruit of season and promise of promotion to 'ordinary seaman at end of voyage.

Made second voyage in her, presumably as Ordinary Seaman. By G.R.M's account vessel made no further voyages. After suffering from storm in Bay

COMMODORE, Capt. Nance. Capt. Nance. c1847/48

Once again, several possible vessels none of which have Capt. Nance shown as being in command. I believe the most like is a schooner built at Newport in 1834, commanded by a Capt. Barnes. There is a connection with the HERALD as the owners were Matthews and Co of Penzance who subsequently owned that schooner. It does seem possible that Capt Nance was a favourite of those owners and did have command at the time GRM sailed on her.

Both of these vessels were generically known as 'fruit schooners, designed for speed in order to carry perishable cargo. They were nearly always 'topsail schooners', meaning that they had square topsails on the fore-mast. George confirms this for the COMMODORE with his reference on p.26.

Shipwrecks and Bush Felling

Voyage to Gibraltar, Spain and then in ballast to Messina to load sulphur and raisins.

Vessel was caught up in the power struggle between Britain, France and Spain prompted by France breaking an agreement when they allowed the Bourbon princess Luisa Fernanda to marry the Dauphines son in October 1846. At the same time Sicily was struggling to gain independence from the Bourbon rulers in Italy. 1847/48 were unsettled and violent years across Europe. I don't know enough of the history to judge whether the British Consul would be helping a Bourbon princess escape the mob but we did have an interest. Britain's concern was to maintain a clear passage through the Mediterranean.

This voyage illustrates how improving communications was changing the business of ship owning. Once a ship set off on a long voyage it usually fell to the master to find any subsequent cargoes. Capt. Nance did do this at Gib as well as arranging the necessary ballast. However, since 1835 P & O had been operating fast and reliable mail service to Gib and the Mediterranean. So the owner was able to fix a cargo of sulphur from Messina in London and communicate the fact by letter to Capt Nance in time for him to sail for Messina.

CHATHAM, 1854. There seems to be a gap in his seafaring career

Barque, 354tons, built Liverpool 1825. Owners Jameson of Liverpool. L.R. gives Capt. as Morrison.
Able Seaman.
Uneventful nine month voyage on Government service to West Indies and back to London.

G.R. Meredith / W.E. Hamilton

UNNAMED Barque.

Run from London to Cardiff with a cargo of wheat. 'Paid wages ahead of time' cf. p35.

Vessel leaked causing the grain to swell and split the vessel in two. Sunk conveniently off the 'Newport' lighthouse, within a few miles of Bristol. It must have been the West Esk lighthouse, at that time on an island but now surrounded by reclaimed farmland. It also seems unlikely that the grain would have swollen enough to split the vessel on such a short voyage.

The circumstances, particularly wages being paid in advance, suggest that perhaps the owner was involved in some kind of insurance fraud. On the other hand the cargo may have been rejected by the original consignees on arrival in London because of its damp condition and less particular purchasers had been found in Bristol. In that case GRM would have been part of a run crew signed on to take the vessel there. But in either case the vessel must have been barely seaworthy when she sailed from London.

1849/50 (missed signing on *LADY GRANT* of London bound for New Orleans with railway iron and which was subsequently lost with all hands)

LADY WEST of London, a large barque also bound for New Orleans with 2000 tons of railway iron.

Unable to trace these vessels.

Cargo shifted in Bay and punctured hull. Seven days adrift in lifeboat. Rescued by the Esher of Liverpool and landed at Falmouth.

Shipwrecks and Bush Felling

PRINCE, Capt. Thomas.   1854.

Snow brig, 268 tons, built Scilly Isles 1848, owned by Richards and Registered in Plymouth.

There seems to be a gap in his seafaring career after the loss of the LADY GRANT but we do have a firm date for this voyage.

Twelve-month Voyage to Algoa Bay to load wool.

Fall from aloft resulted in injury. Was well nursed on board if by rather primitive means. While there witnessed the loss of the troopship ***CHARLOTTE,*** 19th Sept 1854. 117 lost, including 26 children. Full details can be found on line at
https://www.pdavis.nl/Charlotte.php.

STAR.

Signed on in London to join in Liverpool but deserted before she sailed

LANCE American ship. Ex slave runner. Contract to carry cattle to Guadeloupe.

Not traced.

AEROLITE Capt. J. Downie.

Barque, 423 tons. Built and registered in Fraserborough 1853. Owned by Wemys & Co. bound for Melbourne

The AEROLITE'S maiden voyage appears to have been to Perth rather than Melbourne so he probably sailed on her second or third voyages in 1855/56.

Jumped ship on arrival at Melbourne and began his career in Australia and New Zealand. This was not unusual at that

G.R. Meredith / W.E. Hamilton

time. Masters expected to sign-on a new crew after a long stay in an Australian port.

Other vessels mentioned in the narrative:

HACKFIELD of Melbourne, Capt. Travers.

JANE FLETCHER 1857

Coastal steamer *LADY JANE*

Emigrant ship *CRESSWELL* , arr. Lyttleton 17th sept. 1859

Barque, Capt. Barnett. 515 tons. Built Sunderland 1849. Owner Tebbutt & Co. Reg. London

STRATHALLAN, Capt. Tod
Ship, 548 tons. Built Dundee 1857. Owner Young & Co. Surveyed 1859 for a voyage Dundee to N.Z.

Descendents

George Richard MEREDITH
Birth: 1 Sep 1834 Place: Crown St., Finsbury, Shoreditch, London
Death: 1 Dec 1918 Place: Waimate, Sth,. Canterbury, New Zealand.
Burial: 3 Dec 1918 Place: Waimate Cemetery, Sth Canterbury, New Zealand
Occupation: Sawmiller & Quarryman
Father: John Richard MEREDITH '(1792-1873)
Mother: Mary Ann (Marian) WELLS (1798-1868)
Marriage: 15 Sep 1859 Place: Reg. Off., Lyttleton, Cant., New Zealand

Wife: Jessie FERGUSSON
Birth: 19 Nov 1837 Place: Dowally, Dunkeld, Perthshire, Scotland
Death: 6 Aug 1921/1922 Place: Rangi Maru, Waimate, Sth. Canterbury, New Zealand

G.R. Meredith / W.E. Hamilton

Burial: Place: Waimate Cemetery, Sth. Canterbury, New Zealand
Comments: 'Jessie!-Is The Same Name As 'Janet'
Father: Donald (Daniel) FERGUSSON (1806-1887)
Mother: Catherine ANDERSON (1819-1879)

Children
1. M Child: George MEREDITH
Birth: 10 Aug 1860 Place: Kakahu, Sth. Canterbury, New Zealand
Death: 10 Feb 1907 Place: Geraldine, Sth. Canterbury, New Zealand. Aged 47 Yrs.
Burial: Place: Geraldine, Sth. Canterbury, New Zealand.
Spouse: Janet SMITH
Marriage: Oct 1882

2. F Child: Catherine Anne (Kate) MEREDITH
Birth: 3 Jan 1862 Place: Kakahu, Sth. Canterbury, New Zealand
Death: 16 Mar 1942 Place: Waimate. Sth Canterbury, New Zealand
Burial: Place: Waimate Cemetery, Sth Canterbury, New Zealand
Spouse: John Matthew BUTCHER
Marriage: 4 Feb 1880 . Place: Geraldine, South Canterbury, New Zealand

Shipwrecks and Bush Felling

3. M Child: Athol Richard MEREDITH
Birth: 23 Jun 1863 Place: Pleasant Valley, Kakahu, Sth. Canterbury, New Zealand
Death: 11 Oct 1946 Place: Public Hospital, Stratford, From Toko
Occupation: Sawmiller
Comments: 'Athole' On Birth Certificate
Spouse: Amy Flora (Cecille) SIMMONS
Marriage: 2 Oct 1895 Place: Stratford, Taranaki, New Zealand

4. F Child: Jessie MEREDITH
Birth: 12 Sep 1864 Place: Kakahu, Fairfield, Sth. Canterbury, NZ
Death: 25 Jul 1961 Place: Stratford. Taranaki, New Zealand
Spouse: Wlliam McLaughlin KENNEDY
Marriage: 15 Feb 1884 Place: Geraldine, Sth. Canterbury, New Zealand

5. F Child: Marlon MEREDITH
Birth: 30 Jun 1866 Place: Kakahu, Sth. Canterbury, New Zealand
Death: 8 Aug 1951
Burial: Place: Timaru, Sth. Canterbury, New Zealand
Spouse: . Alexander HERON
Marriage: 18 Apr 1892

G.R. Meredith / W.E. Hamilton

6. F Child: Christina (Tina) MEREDITH (No Family)
Birth: 14 May 1868 Place: Kakahu, Sth. Canterbury, New Zealand
Death: Place: In England
Spouse: Lawson WEBB
Marriage: 1921

7. F Child: Eva MEREDITH, Dr (No Family)
Birth: 18 Dec 1869 Place: Kakahu, Sth. Canterbury, New Zealand
Death: 17 Apr 1946 Place: Edinburgh, Scotland
Occupation: Doctor Of Medicine
Spouse: W H CLEMENTS Dr

8. F Child: Alice MEREDITH Dr
Birth: 3 Jun 1871 Place: Kakahu, Sth. Canterbury, New Zealand
Death: 10 Apr 1949 Place: Bangor, County Down, Northern Ireland
Occupation: Doctor Of Medicine
Spouse: David William Murray BURN M.A.
Marriage: 29 Mar 1888 Place: Geraldine, South Canterbury, NewZealand

9. M Child: James MEREDITH (Died Early)
Birth: 28 Mar 1873 . Place: Georgetown, Canterbury, New Zealand
Death: 29 Oct 1873
Occupation: Infant

Shipwrecks and Bush Felling

10. F Child: Eliza MEREDITH (Died Early)
Birth: 29 Sep 1874 Place: Temuka, Sth. Canterbury, NZ
Death: 24 Apr 1875
Occupation: Infant

11. M Child: Charles MEREDITH
Birth: 12 Dec 1876 Place: Kakahu, Geraldine, Sth. Canterbury, New Zealand
Death: 13 Apr 1960 Place: Cambridge, Waikato, NewZealand
Spouse: Annie May Sarah (Bird) TAYLOR
Marriage: 18 Jun 1912 Place: Cambridge, Waikato, New Zealand

12. M Child: Samuel Ernest (Sam) MEREDITH
Birth: 2 Oct 1877 Place: Kakahu, Sth. Canterbury, New Zealand
Death: 7 Dec 1944 Place: Palmerston North, New Zealand
Spouse: Anna (Molly) GREEN
Marriage: 28 Sep 1904 Place: New Plymouth, Taranaki, New Zealand

13. M Child: William Edward (Will) MEREDITH
Birth: 20 Dec 1878 Place: Kakahu, Geraldine, Sth. Canterbury, New Zealand
Death: 30 Mar 1965 Place: Public Hospital, Taumarunui
Burial: 2 Apr 1965 Place: Taumarunui
Occupation: General labourer
Comments: No Surviving Children
Spouse: Emily (Peg) GREEN

G.R. Meredith / W.E. Hamilton

Marriage: 18 Sep 1907 Place: Registrar's Office, New Plymouth

14. M Child: John Thomas MEREDITH
Birth: 23 Aug 1880 . Place: Kakahu, Geraldine, Sth .. Canterbury, New Zealand
Death: 20 Jun 1954 Place: Timaru, Sth. Canterbury, New Zealand
Burial: 22 Jun 1954 Place: Soldiers' Portion, Boer War, Timaru Cemetery, Cant., NZ
Occupation: Cycle and Motor Mechanic
Spouse: Eveline Mary GRIFFITHS
Marriage: 13 Aug 1903 Place: Residence E Griffith, Hilton, 8th. Cant., N.Z. Separated

Shipwrecks and Bush Felling

About the Author

Wendy Hamilton is George Richard's great, great, granddaughter. She comes down through the line of his youngest son John, whose son was Frank. Frank was the father of Shirley, Wendy's mother. George Meredith's manuscript fell into Wendy's hands through Shirley's cousin Rex Livingstone.

What makes the writing of this book so significant to Wendy, is prior to this she knew nothing of the Meredith branch of the family, other than they came from Timaru. Although Shirley remembers her father faithfully writing to his parents every week, he never once spoke of them. The one thing we do know, is the marriage was not a happy one like George and Jessie's marriage, for it ended in separation. To discover a forefather as adventurous and brave as George has been a delight for Wendy. His voice comes out strong and cheerful in his writing. To find he was a man who trusted God was like uncovering buried treasure.

This is the first historical book Wendy has worked on and she hopes it won't be her last. Through it she has discovered she loves researching history

G.R. Meredith / W.E. Hamilton

Other Books By Wendy Hamilton

<u>Eating a Light Bulb does not make you Bright</u>
Light on Home-schooling
<u>I told you not to Climb the Cactus.</u>
Surviving the Badlands of Motherhood
<u>Darling the Window is on Fire</u>
Love and House Renovations in New Zealand
<u>Homemade Church</u>
<u>Surviving Home-Schooling Through the Corona Crisis</u>

Children's Books

<u>The Britwhistles win a Prize</u>

<u>The Britwhistles and the Elasticizer</u>

<u>The Unlucky Snails</u>

<u>The Unlucky Snails go to France</u>
<u>Little House in the Bush</u>
Growing Up in New Zealand
<u>Little House in the Cow Paddock</u>
Growing Up in New Zealand

www.ingramcontent.com/pod-product-compliance
Lightning Source LLC
Chambersburg PA
CBHW021102080526
44587CB00010B/347